*PARAMILITARY*

# COVERT OPERATIONS

*INTEGRATED TACTICAL WARFARE SERIES VOL. 3*

# R.J. GODLEWSKI

*Eliminating elitism from defense.*

# TABLE OF CONTENTS

# DEDICATION

*To liberty...once and for all.*

*In veneration of Saint Joseph, soft spoken protector of the Holy Family and eternal "Terror of Demons". Scripture records no words from your lips, but your mission ensured the salvation of the human race...Thank you!!!*

## ACKNOWLEDGMENTS

To God the Father, the Son, and the Holy Spirit, without Whom I would find no talent, no opportunity, and no friends with which to affect either my trade or my interests.


*Deo gratias.*

# CHAPTER ONE:
INVISIBLE WARFARE.

SUN-TZU WROTE that deception was the foundation of warfare in that success rested upon creating illusions to thwart the spies and commanders of the enemy. When one was strong, he was advised to act weak. When weak, perhaps, to exhibit strength. If an army was advancing towards the north, preparations suggesting a trek towards the south were advised. Similarly, if an attack was planned for the night hours, all suggestions would lead an enemy to prepare for one during daylight. For the Chinese tactician and general, war left no certainties for an enemy to digest.

Covert operations build upon this principle by removing the identifiable aspects of warfare through forces shielded from the aggressor. In other words, deception to the point of invisibility – a practice immortalized within Japan's infamous ninjas, who evolved along the lines of ninjutsu or the art of stealth and invisibility. Nevertheless, these thorns within the side of "respectable" contemporaries such as the samurai class remained far less organized than, say, the *real* assassins of the Middle East.

The Nizar'ilyya sect of the Islamic heretic known simply as the "Old Man of the Mountain" took assassination to its most sinister and – for lack of more appropriate words – industrial level. Preferring to use knives or daggers rather than any "standoff" weapons available, the Assassins spent months and years penetrating the inner circle of their targets, posing as monks, scribes, servants, and whatever function permitted them to reach the personal space of the victim.

Where both ninja and Assassin equally failed, however, rests with the identity of their function; mention either term – even centuries later – and everyone understands *whom* you are referencing. For all their diversity and capabilities, both ninjas and their Nizar'ilyya brethren were killers – nothing more, nothing less. In the case of the former, they were literally cooked alive in boiling oil if they were ever caught.

Functional covert operations, ideally, leave presence to the imagination. That is, even if caught, covert operators remain undisguisable from the locals. Or so the theory should suggest. Unfortunately, the mere term *covert* has been diluted through practice and obfuscated by bureaucratic governments in the same manner as soldiers of fortune – history's true mercenaries – have been termed out of existence by the presence of "private military companies" or "private security companies". Again, everyone knows a rose even if presented by another name, but functionality itself can be quite deceiving.

From here, we can detect the very nature of warfare's greatest vice: leaving battle to bureaucrats to officiate. In the cyclic nature of human evolution, inability leads to need, which then allows opportunists to arise for the riches to be had, followed shortly by legislators seeking to profit themselves through law and apparent order. All this supposed "progress" simply provides is more fodder for conflict and mayhem, intensifying the planet's appetite for war and participants to offer a better mousetrap for destruction.

As both nations – and hostilities – grow and divide, conflict becomes ever more localized, even if modern technology allows the remotest of battles to emerge as newsworthy events across the globe. To keep a disinterested public tuned in, these broadcasts eagerly illuminate singular casualties and ignore the fact that warfare has been around for as long as two siblings walked the planet. Aggravated by this "marketing" of conflicts, politicians and tyrants both seek to shield themselves through covert operations and, presently on the rebound, the privatization of war through independent contractors acting as either proprietors or corporations.

## The Essence of Being Paramilitary

Given a free and open market, whatever governments provide can be offered – more often than not at greater efficiency – by private entities emancipated from red tape and micromanagement. These smaller, more innovative and entrepreneurial providers can whisk past the bungling nature of "too big to succeed" institutions and target the heart of any problem, be it social, commercial, or aggressive in nature. In this regard, perhaps, civilization rests upon the common sense of individuals whose heretofore lack of "credentialization" merits an objective look at the world's problems.

As language often contains a historical record of human activity and thought, it also provides confirmation of the discussion of what necessarily comes first – the institutional chicken or the individual egg. Words do not arise *until* there is a subject to be defined and, more often than not, well appreciated. Authors of fantasy novels, to illustrate the point, often struggle to describe fictional environments, races, and events. What might be readily discernable within his or her mind remains absolutely foreign for the newly acquired reader. It is only after a great deal of success do such unfamiliar words enter into the public lexicon.

The very same progression holds true for industry.

Rarely, if ever, do governments fashion a need for a service or product until it has been developed and practiced within the private sector. Nor do they reliably develop that product or service without, at the very minimum, substantial influence from that private sector. Part of this results from individuals carrying personal beliefs and experiences *into* government for absorption by that institution. Another avenue remains that as populations grow and taxpayer-funded resources dwindle, governments, again, turn towards more productive and efficient solutions to keep its handle on an ever more powerful constituency.

In the world of security and military operations, the discussion encapsulates both *officially endorsed* activity and that provided by – or offered to – independent entities. Here is where the term "paramilitary" offers itself – *para* in meaning similarity to, and *military* involving martial actions taken to impose influence or deny such through defensive measures. For our discussion, paramilitary refers to either government operations undertaken in a manner similar to existing military activities (such as when the U.S. Drug Enforcement Administration engages hostile narcotics trafficking organizations) or completely private affairs such as when those drug trafficking entities combat competitors or local police agencies.

Whichever the case, paramilitary operations imply those activities that rest upon military-style organization, equipment usage, and, for our purposes, martial response to societal problems. Personnel need not be segregated into identified ranks nor does equipment employed have to be military issue (merely employed within similar functions). Rather, the emphasis remains unit discipline and strategic or tactical planning. In the broader public, organizations tend to lack both such insight and devotion.

Although paramilitary operations can be affected by either governments or private organizations, this book will focus upon the latter, suggesting that *private* military functions serve more effectively than, say, national institutions whose more official military operations leave much to be desired. In other words, if a nation fails its standing military, it may further fail the essence of possessing private military functions.

In consideration of this, our view of paramilitary functions distances the activity from *conventional* military theory and doctrine; the essence of employing paramilitary forces suggesting that either personnel or equipment remains lacking. This, of course, does *not* suggest that either need be of inferior quality. In fact, many "para" functions tend to remain more professional than their more institutionalized partners. For instance, in many situations, *para*medics may operate more productively and efficiently than his or her hospital-based compatriots despite the latter possessing more resources.

Furthermore, paramilitary functions imply a stronger desire to adapt and innovate solutions that bureaucratic armies and navies cannot produce. Moreover, many of these private functions arise to meet needs more localized than those encountered by larger forces – such as the aforementioned DEA agents raiding a drug laboratory, yet more private in function. Consider the employment of an executive protection detail safeguarding a corporate client; their movements, training, and professionalism speak of vast military experience, but their role remains very focused and precise.

To succeed within any endeavor, paramilitary organizations must adhere to the following rules:

1 The group must be disciplined, trained, and practiced for all conceivable contingencies;

2 Individuals within the group must be intelligent, practical, observant, and punctual;

3 Equipment employed by the group must be

modern, functional, and minimal;

4 Organization of the group must be streamlined, decentralized, and accountable.

You will note that *none* of these attributes are noticeably military in scope. That is, they remain valid for a wide range of industries from security and emergency medical services on through corporate marketing and transportation management. This is ostensibly because being "militant" and "war fighting" remain two distinct activities.

Today, one would *not* consider the Roman Catholic Church, as but one example, to be a warfighting organization, yet its presence here on earth remains officially called the "Church Militant" for its desire to have adherents endure the fight for salvation. Similarly, the Salvation Army is decidedly an "army", ripe with officers of varying ranks and uniforms. Yet, again, no one would consider the Army an actual military fighting organization.

This trend towards avowed militancy and diverted aggression underscores another subject containing elements of both warfighting and peace; *covert* operations – the ability to function without any direct connection to the affairs at hand. In other words, to conduct without being culpable for the actions of the task. Although not necessarily a military operation, covert actions are generally considered the exclusive domain of federal governments. This assessment is faulty.

## Defining Covert

Covert operations, for the ease of discussion, represent those activities for which the perpetrator seeks to absolve him or herself from legal, moral, and public scrutiny arising from that activity. As opposed to *clandestine* operations, wherein the practitioner is immediately discovered if caught, covert operations remain deeply secretive with multiple layers of deception to keep prying eyes from discerning the perpetrators. Moreover, colloquially speaking, covert operations generally involve groups or organizations rather than individuals.

To illustrate the nature of covert action to its fullest level, one must borrow from theology. The concept of spiritual beings – either angels or demons – suggest created intelligences that, bearing no corporeal bodies, are not limited by the physical laws of nature that confound human beings. Their role, as determined through historical theology, rests with aiding (angels) or preventing (demons) individuals from achieving salvation in heaven following that person's death. In this regard, *no one* can determine whether a person is so being aided or prevented because spirits cannot be observed by human eyes. That is, for example, an individual can never really know if his or her sins were caused by the temptations of a devil or through his or her own prevalence to sin. The effect is, of course, that any spirits that *do cause mischief* remain unknown and incapable of being charged with the crime.

From the earthlier perspective, forensic evidence will always allow for chance discovery of covert operatives, but the professionals will diminish this probability through layers of cover and deception, more to engage security through attrition rather than shield any participation. When most modern nations ascribe to some measure of 'rule of law' and 'due process', covert action simply means presenting enough doubt as to prevent the practitioner from direct identification with the action for which covert activities are warranted.

Therefore, covert operations remain more about a lifestyle than merely an opportunistic endeavor and this, perhaps more than anything else, solidifies the role of groups within these operations, for only groups can provide the myriad of security, operational, logistical, and financial considerations that go into blending martial behavior in with plausible deniability.

From the paramilitary perspective, feigning military operations *and* hiding the group's participation within these militant activities proceed hand in hand. Often, the group undertaking the mission represents but a series of compartmentalized assets that sometimes suggest governmental involvement and sometimes betray private participation (always providing "clues" towards both keeps outsiders guessing).

Here we shoulder the value of covert action: the slightest hint of doubt fosters continual investigation. To understand this, we can draw upon a key episode from the Second World War. While not directly covert in nature – the Germans knew *precisely* who orchestrated the stunt – the issue of doubt remains of paramount importance. To deceive the enemy, the Royal Air Force literally dropped one of military history's most illustrative hoaxes upon a vaunted Nazi airbase: a helium-filled soccer ball covered with luminescent paint.[1]

The hovering, drifting, bouncing, and *glowing* ball soon had every German in the vicinity scurrying for the shelters as they considered that, perhaps, the strange object was *supposed to be shot at.* Knowing that a single, exceptionally brave pilot had risked life and limb to drop the device, all but the most stoical individual fumbled with explanations for what the "super-secret" weapon would do to them. For two whole weeks, Nazi scientists analyzed the device until they reached a consensus opinion: Germany had been duped. The secret weapon was merely a product of not-so-secret British humor. Nazi leadership was not so accommodating, however, and ordered further examinations.

The object lesson here, of course, is that doubt can be

---

[1] Hadley, Arthur T. "Maneuver Warfare and the Art of Deception" in *Maneuver Warfare: An Anthology* ed. Richard D. Hooker, Jr. (Novato, CA: Presidio Press, 1993), 360-372.

extremely disarming. Who would have – *could* have – believed that the British would risk a life just to drop a glowing soccer ball upon a well-protected German airfield? Yet, the ruse worked; an entire Nazi organization and, especially, its leadership had taken precious time and resources away from the war to examine a hoax. Perhaps mirror-imaging their own omnipotent hierarchy, the Germans simply could not foresee a time when the "master race" could be so stupefied by one of humanity's oldest slogans: "Gotcha!"

If, however, Great Britain and Germany had *not* been at war and the aircraft dropping the ball upon an airfield was not *marked* as an enemy airplane, what could have been the result? Would the initial terror have been worse or less? Imagine following the September 11, 2001 attacks in New York and Washington if an unidentified aircraft had dropped a glowing device upon a city center. How massive would the response have been? Would the device be scrutinized under explosive, chemical, or biological threat conditions?

In the context of our discussion, "covert" means an ability to conduct a mission, operation, or otherwise influence individuals or groups *without* being exposed as the culprit. As such, covert warfare delves deeply into *invisible* warfare, far more lethal than simply so-called "black operations" that are almost exclusively the domain of government forces. Invisible warfare shepherds in a range of invisible warriors, organizations, and agendas.

## Patterns of Invisibility

Given the nature of covert operations, it bears much value to define the various concepts of remaining incognito within these activities. To understand the differing employment and expectations of operating *invisibly* amongst a given population – whether friendly or enemy – we need to analyze the various considerations of what "invisibility" means in the context of paramilitary operations and how each element portends advantage.

- *Physical invisibility.* In this context, it means that soldiers and other individuals can move through a particular environment without being observed by adversarial forces. Too often, minor details within an individual's clothing, uniforms, equipment, or mannerisms betray his or her existence. Camouflage merely *covers* the presence of these things; true invisibility requires that their presence goes unnoticed without concealment. To walk amongst bears, for instance, and appear as if just another member of the den.

- *Operational invisibility.* Operational invisibility simply means that one's actions are not detected as foreign to that particular environment. If, say, a baseball pitcher was to start calling out instructions to what he perceived to be a wide receiver positioned beyond a net, then one would quickly realize that this "athlete" was mentally absorbed in three different sports. Nevertheless, many "professionals" make similar mistakes, even if they may not be as noticeable to untrained eyes. Covert operations require an individual to function within the environment and not simply blend into it. More appropriately, to move *with* the environment rather than simply move *through* it.

- *Associative invisibility.* The adage states that people are only as good as the company he or she keeps. Nowhere is this more valid than within the world of covert operations – with a slight proviso. If one were walking through a group of very hostile individuals, then that person must be as hostile as the others. Mere "attitude" may not be as effective for local populations can quickly ascertain the presence of others even if the intruders "act" as malignant. This can be observed, for instance, by watching a Hollywood film depicting a true story (especially if it remains a war movie). Often, the professional actors remain as incompatible with the professional soldiers as to make many film directors avoid showing images of the *real* heroes. One may *act* like a killer, for example, but a *true* killer bears an unmistakable look about him or her.

- *Mental invisibility*. Building upon the above, few individuals can muster the raw courage and mental attitude to equate with, say, a group of hardened narcoterrorists or Islamic jihadists. A Westerner, for one, would find it difficult to parade amongst of group of Taliban soldiers beheading children merely for studying within school. The slightest flinch of an eyelid may spell doom for his or her covert status. And, yet, this very same individual may next have to parade amongst a group of more civilized people *without* betraying his or her ability to slit throats with ease.

These attributes of invisibility cross government, corporate, social, religious, and entrepreneurial lines.

Even within commerce, the ability to deceive and blend into groups remains important, particularly within the field of industrial espionage. Economic spies must conduct his or her function with complete secrecy lest they sacrifice their client to a pantheon of legal, moral, and legislative crises. Detection can mount from the slightest error in judgment, perception, or mannerism.

Success within covert endeavors requires the operation to remain as invisible as possible to potential adversaries *and* curious observers. While most of the human population does not necessarily pay close attention to his or her surroundings, almost *every* individual will notice trespassers due to inherent xenophobia. When casual observation may lead to capture or death, invisibility becomes the fantasy for which both Hollywood and the defense industry strive. Yet, properly trained, conditioned, and motivated personnel can achieve a facsimile of the "superhuman".

## Summary

Warfare remains the martial implementation of deception. To succeed on the battlefield requires keeping adversaries guessing as to your intentions and capabilities. Such innovation and deception, lauded by governmental agencies, arises from the minds and talents of entrepreneurial individuals that can build a better mousetrap for combat operations. Often, these "paramilitary" activities prepare the way for covert operations – invisible warfare at its finest – and herein lays the need for a fundamental realignment in how military forces function. To win wars by serendipitously confusing the enemy and shielding oneself from the civilian population.

# CHAPTER TWO:
## DIRTY WARFARE, NASTY BASTARDS.

THE FUNDAMENTAL REASON to escape culpability remains that the individual or group in question seeks to hide some measure of indiscretion within that activity. To fight remains as natural for humanity as being born kicking and screaming. To fight *dirty* remains as natural as padding one's resume for an important job interview. At our most primal level, individuals will do *whatever it takes* to emerge victorious over our rivals, whether that entails deflating footballs for a better grip or abusing steroids for larger muscles. To consider people as "fair" violates 25,000+ years of building civilization.

When King Edward III unleashed gunpowder upon the European continent for the very first time, the English monarch was not thinking about international norms or ratified treaties. The belligerent opportunist was striving to win at all costs and employing a literal "game changer" did not violate his conscience. After all, wars were brutal, bloody, and quite frequent during the era of the Hundred Years' War. Nevertheless, Edward's innovation – if not invention – shook modern warfare with a thunderous vibration that would never abate. Warfare had become overt on a historical scale.

National militaries seem to thrive on loudness and disruption; the larger, the more massive the armament, the greater prestige accorded to that nation's army. This has been true from the largest bombard of antiquity on through the Soviet Union's absolutely psychotic 50-megaton hydrogen blast. Even al-Qaeda's attacks on 9/11 were intended to literally shake towering office buildings – and America's psyche – to the ground. Regardless, such ostentatious displays of "thunder and roar" – or far more recently, "shock and awe" – do little but announce the presence of militaries and availing presence is what sometimes leads to disaster.

Secrecy, for its role, does some good in diminishing the acknowledgement of *where* militaries arrive. The D-Day invasion of 6 June 1944 provides a solid example. The Nazi regime *knew* that the Allies were coming; they could *see* the thousands of troops massed within Great Britain. They just did not know, for certain, where and precisely when those tens of thousands of fresh troops would land. The noise associated with preparing for history's greatest invasion was effectively diluted through absolute secrecy.

In another psyche-testing military campaign, Joshua's Israelites marched around Jericho seven times before they blew their horns, cried aloud, and stormed in through the city's crumbling walls.[2] This act had been presaged by six days of similar maneuvering, but the terrified residents of Jericho had no idea *when* the final assault would take place because only the Israelites knew the day. The besieged citizens of Jericho only knew that an attack was coming and, possibly, even where.

Relatively speaking, both the Israelites enveloping Jericho and the Allies traumatizing Germany during the Second World War represented the largest military forces of their environment. Their purpose was hardly a secret; they existed to punish the enemy and pound him into submission. Covert operations, much to the contrary, keep enemies awake at night through their very *potential* – the prospects of being attacked by *any* force traumatizes, but attack from

---

[2] Joshua 6:1-27, *New American Bible*.

"ghosts" keeps even warriors lying in bed with one eye open and one hand on a dagger (or firearm).

Even the greatest of military tacticians are unnerved by the professed ability of an adversary to "...strike where we want when we want – and nobody can stop us."[3] Who, after all, can defend against an apparition? Who can foresee an assault from a phantasm? From where do ghosts *truly* arise from? In the modern age, to defend against a threat that can enter your protective sphere from any literal position – sky, sea, land, cyber, psychological, political – remains a thorn within the side of both tactical and strategic planners.

## Unconscionable Warfare

War, as a human activity, remains exclusively the realm of death and destruction; to kill and/or destroy. It is *not* the domain of exerting one's political influence any more than it remains to aid the disadvantaged in building civic infrastructure or tending to the sick (these being, perhaps, the exclusive domain of religion). The sole function of militaries remains the capability to "crush, kill, and destroy" one's martial opponents. War simply represents the manifestation of that desire to obliterate enemy forces, whether enacted officially or otherwise.

Largely before recorded history, warfare represented mankind's most violent and unrestrained passion. Within its filial, tribal perspective, war represented the continuation of the clan through personal combat and literal decimation of human bodies. Weapons were crude, bone and skull crushing instruments that extended the attributes of human muscle through sheer dynamics of physics: momentum and mass combined to pulverize the calcium-reinforced collagen that keeps human beings standing erect.

Even as weapons of war became more refined, more "surgical" within their ability to cut through human bone and tissue, their employment still retained the sense of primal barbarism that shuddered the mind of the weak and timid. Larger, sharper blades cut more effectively and repeatedly. Larger, more powerful bombs extended the radius of lethal shrapnel. More engineered, more quality-controlled rifles ended up shattering skulls thousands of meters away. Nuclear weapons, even of the crudest variety, swept entire cities off the map.

Perhaps Hollywood films led to the desensitization of the public regarding the reality of war. First, censorship kept older movies from being too graphic for sensitive minds. Later, computer graphics depicted extreme violence as almost too comical to be believed. Society moved from antiseptic motion pictures towards sarcastically depicted explosions and martial arts scenes. War, however it remains displayed within the media, is most emphatically *not* choreographical; no mere script – or master plan of battle – could ever hope to encompass its myriad of inconceivable consequences.

At best, warfare is governed through the creativity inherent within both the aggressor and the defender, knowing that a great deal of "luck" is incorporated into any perceivable outcome. The greater the need for directed violence, the greater the level of creativity rested within the plan of operation. In this regard, covert operations maximize the innovative spirit and creative nature of its participants. That is, with both heart and soul fused into martial campaigns, a creative personality can lead others into combat with an above average expectation for survival.

---

[3] Baylor, Paul, *Manual of the Mercenary Soldier* (Boulder: Paladin Press, 1988), 225.

To understand how creativity may affect battlefield conditions, we must understand how it remains exploited in war.

Eight Methods of Creative Exploitation.[4]

- ***Necessitated Creativity***. This represents innovation caused by a great need or through the lack of required personnel or resources. A group or individual, for instance, may employ civilian pickup trucks to carry heavy caliber weapons as do the Taliban in Afghanistan.

- ***"Drive by" Creativity***. Innovation here is designed to silence adversaries through its sheer brutality and decisiveness. Homicide bombers remain its most illustrative examples, but simple improvised explosive devices, or IEDs, bear similar natures.

- ***Offensive Creativity***. Innovation designed to maintain pressure upon an individual or group and is best exemplified by the "Shock and Awe" campaign of the 2003 invasion of Iraq.

- ***Defensive Creativity.*** To alleviate pressure upon a defender, innovation is employed to change an adversary's plans. This was most notable within the U.S. landing at Inchon during the Korean War.

- ***Psychological Creativity***. As with the aforementioned use of a helium-filled soccer ball by the Royal Air Force, innovation is often employed to disorientate and confuse an adversary.

- ***Technological Creativity***. Modern technology permits

individuals and groups to posturize, or inflate one's abilities to reach broader audiences, whether fully intentional or not. Examples include Orson Welles' 1938 radio broadcast of *War of the Worlds* or more recent Iranian depictions of multiple rocket launches through the use of composite images.

- ***Instructional Creativity.*** Innovation is often used to teach foreign subjects to recruits and students. For example, household goods truck drivers, who must learn to load semi-trailers completely and specifically to ensure safe transport of personal belongings, are confronted with "word puzzles" and Tetris® games to force him or her to imagine outside the box.

- ***Directorial Creativity.*** In order to galvanize individuals or groups into accomplishing the heretofore unthinkable, a leader may employ creative inspiration in the attempt as did President John F. Kennedy during his speech to bring Americans to and from the lunar surface by the end of the 1960s.

Employing these eight basic uses of creative thought, armies and paramilitary forces strive for force multiplication upon the battlefield and tactical, or strategic, advantage.

Within covert operations, however, innovation becomes either a golden shield or an Achilles' heel depending upon whether a military force properly utilizes or misunderstands the subject matter. To succeed, one must employ creative thought as a tool as much as a weapon and engage an enemy at their weakest for it to prove effective (as when the British took the micromanaging Nazis to task with their ruse).

As no military ever went to war with *everything* that it

---

[4] Adopted from Godlewski, R.J. "Latte Intelligence: The Divorce of Shock Creativity and Special Information Operations" in *American Intelligence Journal* 29 no. 1 (2011) 70-79.

needed, creative thought remained necessary to maximize that equipment which it brought into battle. Here is where the duplicity of innovation exists – as either a benefit or as a hindrance to active combat operations. The necessity of combating armored vehicles without military resources, for example, led to the widespread use of Molotov's cocktails and soon anyone with a flammable liquid and a glass container could destroy otherwise unapproachable vehicles. On the other hand, "creativity" within the context of some IEDs ultimately led to the death of the innovator through inexperience and training.

Aside from weapons and other military tools, innovation led to the development and implementation of military tactics and, henceforth, launching wars to begin with. Nazi blitzkrieg doctrine, largely developed through stormtrooper efforts in the First World War, undoubtedly paved the way for Germany's launch of the Second World War in 1939. Had Adolf Hitler not possessed such maneuver warfare troops, it is highly doubted that he would have instigated an attritional style battle against his targets.

Because innovation can lead to martial opportunities, it can escalate those activities beyond the point of "civilized" combat. In other words, creative military *artists* – employing human art for militancy – push the envelope of conventional thought, aggressively seeking implementation of his or her designs for combat as would any other artisan, be they painter, sculptor, or musician. Herein is where war often becomes its bloodiest.[5]

Creative personalities, as with their more analytic science and engineering brethren, see life as a series of problems to be solved. Whereas chemical engineers and physicists, for instance, may search for answers via the

---

[5] Many revolutionaries and political terrorists, if not tyrants such as Hitler, for example, hail from creative backgrounds.

scientific method, creative individuals look for solutions outside the scope of rational human thought. A chemist, say, may fashion IEDs out of common household ingredients, but a more innovative personality learned to employ commercial airliners as very large suicide bombs.

The main problem rests that engineers and scientists remain bound by physical laws; creative personalities, being artists at heart, merely employ the imagination. Here is where a great divergence takes place. Analytical minds, such as scientists and engineers, see their work as more of a cyclic nature than their creative counterparts. An engineer, for instance, may work on a solution only to discover some error in judgement along the way. Then, he or she is likely to cycle back to the original problem and proceed anew.

In contrast, a more innovative spirit may *not* view his or her efforts as part of the problem. Rather, he or she will simply envision *another* goal to attain. The engineer intuitively understands that mathematics, physics, or even available material dictate the outcome. The musician, in contrast, may simply settle with an alternative key to produce his or her song, or a painter may resort to submitting their craft via another color scheme. In this manner, artists remain more unpredictable than engineers, for he or she may not function along avenues easily codified.

When creativity meets martial expression, the results translate into unconventional war. When unconventional war – and its practitioners – are pushed too far, conflict takes upon itself a most unconscionable evolution. Here, again, is where IEDs, punji sticks, money laundering, and cyber attacks gain their foothold within the notoriety of social extremism. Unleashed by human creativity, human misery takes on its own extremes, limited merely by the individual's mind and lack of concern for others.

Warfare becomes ever more brutal, ever "dirtier" in

both its application and its appreciation. When this evolution reaches into the paramilitary field with its pantheon of officials and renegades, martial enterprise erupts from a range of practitioners each eager to disrupt an adversary's plans and formulate strategies to keep rivals at bay. In effect, warfare orchestrated outside the bounds of civility and legality bastardizes what had already been humanity's worst vice.

## Unimaginable Warriors

When Carl von Clausewitz warned, during the early nineteenth century, about excluding "kind-hearted people" from the precepts of national battle, he needn't have worried about paramilitary forces acting within a covert capacity. The combination of unofficial combatants and the secretive nature of warfare beyond the comprehension of others assures that only the most violent, most vicious soldiers emerge upon the asymmetrical battlefield. And for good reason.

The term "soldier" for most of the human population either represents someone forced into service quite ill-prepared for the brutalities of war, or others volunteering for a range of reasons from financial need and gainful employment on through family history and adventure. Almost always, however, the phrase rarely conjures up images of bloodthirsty warriors devoted to winning at any and all costs. Nor is it expected that *all soldiers* are supposed to kill and win wars "at all costs". Only within Hollywood movies are soldiers depicted as superhuman warriors and military hardware devastatingly effective.

Nevertheless, *killing* need not be violent and *soldiers* need not be superhuman in order to startle peaceable people into submission. Most assassinations, for example, remain notoriously quick and often silent. Similarly, the war that devastated a planet and ended with two nuclear detonations saw unpretentious Audie Murphy emerge as the conflict's most decorated hero, credited with singlehandedly killing over 240 enemy soldiers. History swells with the heroics of the nonchalant and quiet.

Inasmuch as people do not wish to see the pain and suffering they inflict upon others – the physical and emotional distances we employ to keep from realizing our culpability[6] – most fear being attacked by the "unknown" more so than being attacked by known threats. Something about the seemingly invisible remains sinister, powering a host of horror movies where the antagonist, if ever visualized, changes appearance at will.

Without a firm "individual" to gain a fix upon, victims and defenders often sensationalize the culprit and marginalize reality. Ordinary strategists such as T.E. Lawrence and bureaucratic organizations such as the Central Intelligence Agency (CIA) become deified through the lens of inconclusive results tainted by extraordinary public appetite. In other words, heroes are often made by those who seek to find heroes. And *true* heroes only emerge after he or she has had a chance to achieve what few others could accomplish.

The same holds true with enemies; the less that we know about them, the more they become *capable* of threatening us. Classic examples include the aforementioned ninja and Assassin cults. Neither groups were particularly special but became notorious through their ability to surprise and create fear amongst their enemies. No one was ever certain whether or not he was an active target of the group, but self-importance kept many a politician and despot awake at night.

---

[6] Grossman, Dave. *On Killing: The Psychological Cost of Learning to Kill in War and Society* (New York: Back Bay Books, 2009), 157.

As with the night encroaching upon a nomad within the desert, the unseen terrifies the uninitiated, and this leads to others becoming terrified through tales and exaggeration. Nevertheless, both Assassins and ninjas were simply warriors operating under the cloak of absolute secrecy. In the case of the latter, they were so vilified by contemporary samurais who demanded a code of conduct for everything from bathing on through how to slice someone with a sword, the mere thought of fighting one's way into a fortress only to find the opposing warlord already killed by a "sneaky" ninja was too much to bear.

The same holds true today with modern elite soldiers – and, especially, the national military leaders that micromanage them – who view their paramilitary brethren with abject disgust. It remains unconscionable for *anyone* to engage within private warfare unless, of course, such paramilitary forces (ostensibly meaning those employed by the CIA, etc.) are staffed with retiring, "loaned", or otherwise discharged military soldiers. *Private* soldiers, even if acting within an obvious security role, become ostracized by the military and demonized by the press. They are today's ninja genetically at odds with today's samurai elite.

The dispersal of commerce, regardless of industry, necessitates a shift away from elitism, cronyism, protectionism, and credentialism. Simply put, the demand remains too great to rely upon people governed by a particular class, owing to an acceptable clan, defined within a specific parameter, or acknowledged by an accredited institution. Yet, the practitioners of commerce *still* gravitate towards acceptability rather than entrepreneurialism. Kings and knights still rule over warriors and businessmen.

Not surprisingly, however, neither kings nor knights represent income-producers; most of their efforts come from *control* and not implementation. A classic example of this involves the exploration of the Americas by the Spaniards and their infamous treasure fleets. For all of their notoriety and scandal, the Spanish crown had very little to do with the mining and transportation of gold and silver beyond monopolistic control over mercury that was required to refine silver.[7] The associated banking, ship operation, even the "security" provided both offshore and on land nestled within the hands of *private* individuals.

These individuals both created and destroyed empires. They improvised and militarized against inconceivable odds and *won* – the Spanish language absolutely dominates the hemisphere, as does Roman Catholicism. They improved upon psychological and special warfare and invented the naval convoy system. And they outlasted their version of Assassins and ninja: pirates. What ultimately doomed Spain – and England, Portugal, etc. – was that these ferocious explorers and soldiers remained very *overt* in their entrepreneurial duties. One simply cannot shape an empire – and terminate others – *without* getting attention.

Although the pirates failed to completely destroy the Spanish exploitation of the New World – England eventually surpassed Spain in global influence – both European monarchies lost way to the rise of militant farmers and other independents seeking liberty. In North America, the United States came into existence largely through the cunning and fieldcraft of farmers and tradesmen, with a few cultured diplomats thrown in for good measure. The heart of the American Revolution, however, centered upon the covert buildup of resentment towards the status quo and an undying belief in the sanctity of the individual person.

Bested by the British in terms of discipline, organization, and logistics, the Americans triumphed through sheer audacity and unconventional tactics. While not

---

[7] Walton, Timothy R. *The Spanish Treasure Fleets* (Sarasota, FL: Pineapple Press, 1994), 38-39.

inventing primal warfare by any stretch of the imagination, the Americans fused such irregular warfare into man's inherent desire to be free and, within a decade, produced what eventually was to become the planet's greatest conventional and special forces military ever. Much of which centered upon *private* – rather than institutional – evolution.

That the United States ultimately had to endure a second war with Britain, savage Barbary pirates, a mind-numbing – and highly industrialized – civil war, Plains Indians, zealous insurgents from the Philippines and Mexico, and two World Wars underscored its ability to adapt to both conventional and unconventional warfare. From this experience and the nation's natural ruggedness arose individuals that toyed with, if not fully appreciated, primitive warfare. As with Great Britain beforehand, the United States won wars largely through sheer size and resources. Yet these, again, represented very messy and overt conflicts.

Governments often fail to produce clean, clandestine wars of the kind that necessitate obscurity and inculpability. The U.S. CIA and its Soviet counterpart, the KGB, tried to outdo one another in revolutionary conflicts, but each side failed to conceal its involvement. What resulted from these paring conflicts, however, was a breed of warrior somewhat familiar with the primal conflicts of prehistory. In other words, soldiers that knew how to fight with makeshift weaponry, fight people bred on tribal hatreds and filial bonding, and endure the worst that nature could unleash upon them. What they lacked, unfortunately, was an ability to function outside popular recognition.

In an age when the CIA and even Israel's heretofore ultra-secret Mossad bear Internet Websites, it remains incredulous that *any* martial operation could proceed without gaining appreciation from outside sources, but popularity can be deceptive in and of itself. As with a magician's sleight of hand routine, activities that garner public (and political) attention shield away from operations that *do* require absolute secrecy.

Along a similar vein, military forces that *appear* special are, more often than not, not really that unique. In fact, a great many "special operations" soldiers are decidedly mundane in every aspect other than appearance. A great many even bearing very *identifiable* tattoos and body piercings; distinguishing features that would help to identify a soldier during capture or recovery.

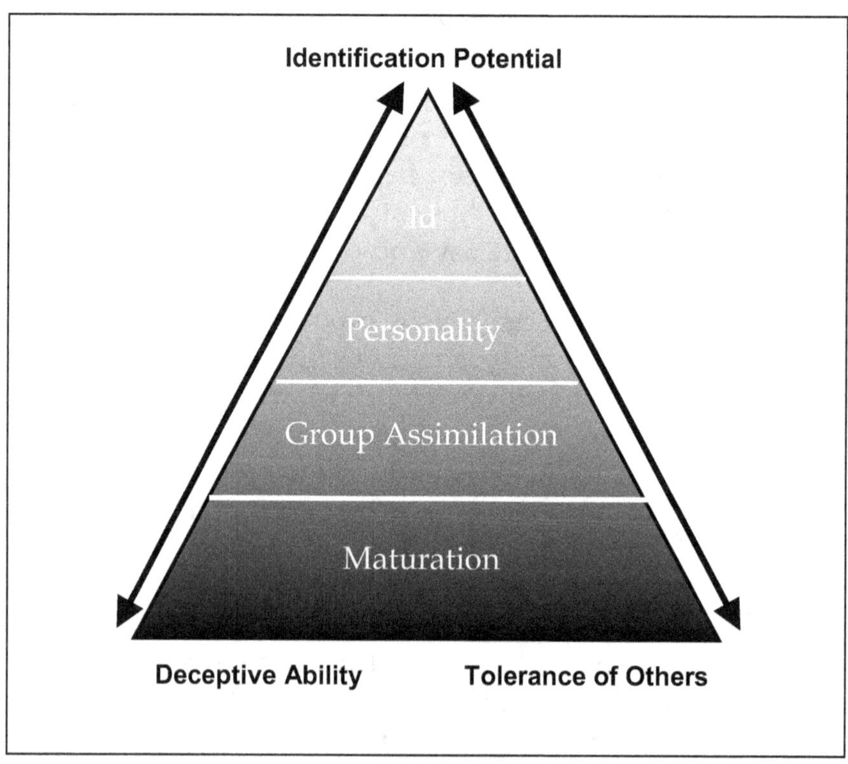


**Figure 1. Pyramid of Personal Identity.** Adapted from Godlewski, R.J "Human Intelligence: Perceiving an Enemy's Thoughts" American Intelligence Journal 27, no 1 (2009), 36.

In Figure 1, we can see how a person's identifiable characteristics are matched against his or her ability to deceive others and blend into distinct groups, based upon that individual's maturity, assimilation towards diverse groups, personality, and his or her "id" – the Freudian third of the psyche that deals with subconscious desires while that person is asleep or unconscious. From this perspective, we can suggest that maturation defines an individual's propensity for tolerating others *and* deceiving them.

Deception and tolerance go hand in hand, for passivity allows an individual to *understand* the target group, fraternize with the crowd, and casually determine a plan of action for deceiving that group. Accordingly, group assimilation itself rests firmly upon this level of maturity. Unfortunately, people are *individuals* and each individual bears a unique personality – even amongst identical siblings. Personalities are what distinguish an individual from *any* group.

For example, one Catholic priest may be authoritative, and employ his pulpit to order his congregation into obedience to the sanctity of Mass. Another priest may be more liberal, even playing guitar and accordion during parish picnics and presenting a more congenial approach to dress and mannerisms in church. Yet, both individuals *are* Roman Catholic priests and bound to the *same laws* governing priests worldwide. That said, the more liberal priest will gain attention for his openness while the conservative priest will be known for enforcing doctrine. Both personalities will distinguish them from the broader Church.

Once personality begins to diversify individuals, the id of the unconscious will seep into both conscious and subconscious mannerisms that may betray a person to others and help to identify him or her. For instance, a devoted musician, while keeping him or herself well grounded into a non-musical assembly, may subconsciously cringe if they hear an off tune note or a disagreeable song. Similarly, a pet lover may subconsciously react to a dog nearly run over by a car in a culture that views animals as mere nuisances.

Such individuals' personality and innermost desires and fears remain more powerful than their broader maturity. In effect, the pyramid in Figure 1 turns upside down; primitive, subconscious thoughts rule his or her actions.

To succeed within paramilitary covert operations, individuals must exist that perform even at the most subconscious level. He or she *must* remain a soldier at heart, a tactician at their very soul, and a warrior beyond all compare. In modernized society, even with its broad depiction of unnatural superheroes on film and video, such personalities remain rare, even unimaginable. Yet, such individuals exist within droves, if not within our national militaries. Perhaps, this is why *para*militarism exceeds beyond the wildest dreams of *pure* militarism.

## Summary

Warfare has always been a violent and chaotic activity, no less so for those that seek to remain hidden from culpability and responsibility. People simply remain focused upon that which he or she deems as worthy of his or her role within the world. Nevertheless, the creative nature of conflict mandates that wars will become exceedingly disruptive and easy to initiate. To shield oneself from public recognition requires individuals to shatter the expectations of group assimilation dynamics and emerge as warriors without 'identity'; that is, soldiers whose deepest psyche permits them to move within their environment rather than through it.

# CHAPTER THREE:


WARS INVOLVING MILITARIES, or even being asymmetrical militarily, necessarily arise the attention of the public, making these conflicts "popular" in scope. On the other hand, if one were to avoid employing national militaries and seeking to shield oneself from the conflict outright, then these more sinister wars would require the participant or participants to disappear into that netherworld of covert and clandestine activity that borders upon the sane world of political expectation and insane world of political opportunism. These conflicts represent the "ghost wars" of both large nations and smaller assemblies.

What they both entail, however, remain conflicts in which one or more aggressors remain outside the code of national governance; wars in which a greater majority of battles take place with little or no public awareness. This is beginning to evaporate within our society of instant data communications and social media platforms, but paramilitary covert actions still succeed on the psychological warfare front. Most importantly, these covert wars trend towards utilizing private contractors outside the realm of traditional paramilitary recruitment efforts; soldiers whose training and experiences do not always reflect compliance.

Technology and social involvement are rapidly diluting the boundaries between commerce, education, social welfare, and, of course, government. For every function offered by a federal or local agency, for example, there are literally dozens of nongovernmental organizations (NGO) offering the same function – and this most emphatically includes both security and military services. At the very minimum, government provision is but an *option* for any foreseeable solution.

Involving what has traditionally been termed "Fourth-Generation Warfare" (4GW) – conflict simultaneously involving operations within the martial, religious, political, and economic sectors – paramilitary operations offer an opportunity to impact any or all of these segments of society through militarily external resources. That is, for example, a nation may be able to influence another's political environment through the use of "amateur soldiers" – soldiers not necessarily formerly trained or financed. When done so covertly, this influence can achieve Clausewitzian political gain without the aggressor government being noticed.

When both paramilitary resources *and* covert operations are employed, war takes upon itself an apparitional nature that borders between declared hostilities and public suspicion. In other words, covert paramilitary operations represent martial conflict on the periphery.

## Goals and Objectives

At their core level, objectives remain simplistic. Whether one is seeking to acquire a billion-dollar corporation, for instance, or a local mom-and-pop diner, the ultimate goal includes the same requisites. The purchaser must first analyze the need for an acquisition or merger, scrutinize viable options, arrangement the necessary funding for the transaction, propose an offer (or intention), and then work to include the acquisition into that purchaser's existing environment. Similarly, goals within war remain the same regardless of the size of the ultimate conflict.

As we have discussed, covert paramilitary operations involve three distinct goals within their objectives: martial application, plausible deniability, and compartmentalization shielding the client – hereinafter meaning any agency or organization controlling the paramilitary group in question. Whatever the objective – assassination of a threatening individual, ambush upon a terrorist or trafficker target, psychological operation, etc. – these goals remain of paramount importance within achieving that end mission.

**Martial application** represents the heart of the operation, for its implementation rests upon militaristic discipline and order. It may not involve an armed mission, per se, but the ultimate aim remains to introduce militancy – if not violence – within its resolution. The previous example of the Roman Catholic "Church Militant" bears this out as adherents are required to literally fight for his or her soul even if defending that particular life with weapons remains unthinkable. It is the *discipline* and struggle that warrants discussion, not the issue of weapons. The goal remains, forever, to *win* in the end.

**Plausible deniability** represents the blanket covering the participants and providers of the operation, which essentially represents the task of remaining invisible to prying eyes. Whereas Catholics making up the Church Militant are necessarily required to proudly voice his or her presence within the world, practitioners of covert paramilitary operations delve deeply into the sinister world of deceit and deception. In essence, a successful operation will lay blame upon *everyone else* rather than those specifically carrying out or endorsing the mission. More specifically, however, plausible deniability represents a "last resort" of sorts should cover for the operation be blown through any number of circumstances. If managed effectively, the covert operation would *not* permit any identification of potential players.

***Compartmentalization*** provides that avenue of secrecy that ensures plausible deniability as a last resort, protective measure. Only those parties *actively* engaged within the covert paramilitary operation would bear knowledge of the mission ensuring that others cannot compromise it. This is accomplished by determining *what specific information is required by those charged with the task of carrying out that function.* For instance, logistical personnel may know what types of firearms are moving through their territory, but they needn't know *who* will use them. Similarly, an accountant overseeing "project" funding need not know *what that particular operation entails* as would, say, an attorney.

At the time of this writing (2018), a contemporary U.S. political example illustrates these three attributes and offers empirical knowledge for the uninitiated. Presently, the political climate within the United States rests ideologically between the liberal, progressive Left and the Conservative Right with the former declaring that Republicans are old-fashioned traditionalists whose policies remain detrimental to modern progress and the latter stating that progressive policies remain disastrous for the economy and personal liberties. More colloquially, this argument pits the heart of America – who care more about food on the table and domestic issues – against "the Swamp" in Washington, D.C. that focuses primarily upon global issues.

Regardless, despite the media heightened hysterics of this Left-versus-Right, Progressive-versus-Conservative fight, the debate itself is decades old and exemplifying the heart of the issue remains the CIA. From its very formation, the CIA leadership "tended to be well-to-do liberal Democrats" who "had grown up in Georgetown a kind of elite within the elite" and who viewed Republicans as "outsiders" who were little more than "cave dwellers" along with the rest of the Capital who espoused traditional values.[8] In other words, the primary national institution for protecting American liberties and security was comprised of people vehemently opposed to the constituency's rights and values.

Understanding this, we can outline the goals and objectives of this political battle within the framework of covert paramilitary operations, using the Progressive Left – arguably America's most aggressive and covert major political body – as our example. As with *any* political institution, the ultimate objective remains absolute power – the ability to establish security for a particular ideology and to hold all others accountable to this system of beliefs. In the case of the liberal Democrats, this ideological objective involves four *specific* goals: abortion on demand, banning firearms, public education, and universal healthcare.

We can now integrate these transitional goals into covert paramilitary's dictums of martial application, plausible deniability, and compartmentalization. In the first field, martial expression, we can easily see how the political Left routinely attacks its opposition. Here, proponents of Progressivism imply that those who do not agree with them are simply too stupid to understand global realities ("Elitism") or remain little more than racist bigots ("Cave Dwellers"). When such accusations fail, members of this sect turn to rousting political opponents from restaurants, protesting at his or her home, and even belittling family members and children. Such activities are very much militant in nature and border upon the excessively violent.

To escape from culpability, Progressive leaders quickly change the public narrative towards others or even offer excuses as to why *they* personally oppose the issues they are promoting for the nation's own good. For example, in the case

---

8 Thomas, Evan, *The Very Best Men: The Daring Early Years of the CIA* (New York: Simon and Schuster, 2006), 99.

of abortion – the undeniable killing of an infant – a liberal politician may offer that he or she is "personally opposed" to the practice, but yet must support it either to protect the woman's life or extend that woman's "right" to procure an abortion. In this narrative, the politician allegedly hates the practice *but is bound to uphold the rule of law* – never minding that he or she actively pursues that particular law. Similarly, whenever *another* public official, say Pope Francis, offers a humble statement that he cannot judge homosexuals, for example, then the Left turns this into the pontiff's endorsement of homosexuality thereby confusing others that, somehow, the Pope is changing two thousand years of Catholic doctrine through a simple – and honest – statement.

These actions further show a preference for compartmentalization amongst progressive operatives. Social media aids in this dramatically as individuals are not only shielded from one another through the Internet, but also their numbers may be inflated through multiple fake account names. This latter element may tempt others into believing that his or her ideas are popular if he or she notices several other "individuals" sharing the same sentiments. Moreover, the relative immunity of the Internet permits political operatives to completely fabricate "news", keeping the momentum towards their ideologies intact. The speed at which information flows during the present ensures that few individuals remain confidant – or knowledgeable – enough to determine what is fact versus what is fabricated.

From this brief political example, we can notice how covert paramilitary operations exist even outside the armed conflict arena. While not necessarily "psychological" in operation, these political activities push to adjust the psychological function of individuals nevertheless. In this regard, they remain covert paramilitary operations owing to their militant discipline, strategic avoidance of culpability, and strong compartmentalization – especially when using pawns who have little clue as to how they are being duped into political confrontation.

## Means and Ends

As with all pursued objectives, paramilitary functions bear both disciplined ends and permissible means. In short, to achieve uncompromising objectives, one must employ uncompromising methods and herein is where covert paramilitary operations excel. Covert operations arise, principally, because all other methods of influence have failed, and the employing organization has determined that fighting dirty ironically requires fighting clean (of culpability). Ordinarily, however, one does not fight dirty if they remain on the "conventional" side of any argument.

People remain a social species and what one is thinking is generally open for introduction whether the group is a small family gathering or a large Website on the Internet. The anonymity of the latter further ensures that restrictions on opinions loosen, particularly through various monikers that keep individuals believing that what remains on the Internet does not stay around for very long. Unfortunately, ideas and thoughts still find a way of locating our adversaries and enemies. From this perspective, those individuals with a more public persona tend to either encapsulate his or her feelings within social media as "policy" or, if the person is a true politician, then he or she will simply cloud the issue in with party ideology.

That people are also a competitive/aggressive species further suggests that we defend our social – and, obviously, political – opinions both competitively *and* aggressively. Here is where honest debate transcends into focused tyranny. We speak of compromise and agreement *only* when the settlement satisfies *our* objectives. In other words, people are always *right* regardless of the opponent.

When those who are in the "right" represent, say, businesses and governments (especially, the "elite of the elite" CIA), then diplomacy truly turns into demand. Secrecy arises, unfortunately, when those who "demand" seeks to hide from diplomacy. For example, a company desiring an acquisition with another firm hostile to the offering may undertake covert actions against the price of the target's stock or the reputation of the target's management. These efforts are likely to reduce the valuation and effectiveness of the takeover and make it easier for the purchaser to offer more "reasonable" solutions. Or at least remove the target as a threatening subject should the acquisition attempt fail.

In this regard, covert paramilitary operations *always* bear a Plan B as an objective. Either the aggressor wants to *control* the target completely, or it wants to *dilute* the target's power and resistance. Again, consider the present (2018) political battle in Washington, D.C. *All* efforts from the political Left seem to focus on either impeaching the current U.S. President (control) or hamper his efforts to lead the nation and prepare for another possible term (dilution). Diluting the reputation and/or success of an adversary is just as effective as the Plan A objective of completely controlling that individual or group.

Because the power-hungry are aggressive at heart, objectives tend to remain more militant than, say, someone eagerly seeking a date with a potential partner. Emotions remain high on both ends, but most individuals simply understand his or her limits and govern their lives accordingly. When the stakes are much higher, then militant behavior – if not armed activity – becomes much more probable. Here is where simple paramilitary martialism takes on its most covert implementation.

When the "ends" is very much non-negotiable, how

savage could the "means" become? This subject has been debated amongst diplomats, tacticians, and college students for centuries. The short answer is, *if* the action under discussion must become covert in nature, *then* the doors are opened completely in regard to precisely *what* may be sanctioned.

Achieving a particular objective becomes an obsession when the means through which that end is achieved do not matter. Consider the above example of seeking a date for instance. Few would aggravate the opportunity through what, today, amounts to stalking. People are generally quitters at heart. Others, however, remain a bit more decisive – and sinister – within their dealings. King David, upon seeing the beautiful Bathsheba bathing, became so infatuated with the woman that he orchestrated – through covert paramilitary means, if you will – her husband Uriah's death upon the battlefield so that the Israelite king could marry her.[9]

How many national leaders have sent soldiers into suicidal situations since? And for less reason. The point being that soldiers and paramilitaries may be sent on missions for which no sane commander could foresee; nor may killing one's own soldier to partake of that man's wife be considered as unethical (as undoubtedly many tyrants throughout the world have done both within the past and presently). The greater the desirous objective, the greater the means will be employed to achieve it.

During the 1960s, Washington's desire to rid itself of the menace known as Fidel Castro grew to the point of considering dropping leaflets advising Cubans that atomic testing had made their air so radioactive as to force them into shaving off their tainted beards in an attempt to humiliate them through thoughts of impotency.[10] Hardly practical, but

---

[9] 2 Samuel 11:1-27, *NAB.*
[10] Thomas, *Very Best,* 207.

obsession rarely is. Neither was sending unsupported and ill-trained paramilitaries to their deaths during the Bay of Pigs invasion. Yet, when the goal was the removal of Castro – only accomplished decades later from his death by (presumably) natural causes – no tactic was deemed too dramatic for consideration.

Nevertheless, this insistency upon completing objectives regardless of cost has hampered military actions throughout the ages. Whether the United States in Vietnam or the Soviet Union in Afghanistan, obsession with the ultimate goal often surpasses the desire to achieve that goal through any means available. As with most human endeavors, the equation levied against practicality sometimes shifts back in its favor as winning becomes too lengthy for transitory individuals to stomach. In this regard, for instance, both the United States and the Soviet Union bore the capacity for wiping their respective adversaries off the map, but the North Vietnamese and Afghans, respectively, fully understood *their* means of achieving their ends: remaining more patient than the U.S. or U.S.S.R.

In this condition, obsession moves away from "at any cost" and, often, dilutes through subsequent objectives (e.g., getting out from lengthy, costly wars). For this reason, paramilitary operations must adhere to the following conditions:

1. Lethality must *not* exceed the means to endure the original objective. By this, we state that the "means" must always balance with the end; efforts must not become an end in and of themselves. If, for instance, the ultimate objective remains the acquisition of a competitor company, then the efforts to purchase that business must *not* irreparably harm the purchaser;

2. Time remains at a premium. Paramilitary operations must address a *specific* goal rather than assume a broader objective; function more tactically rather than strategically. Missions must correspond to recognizable guideposts such as ambushes, targeted killing, rescue efforts, etc. and not undefinable trends as "winning the hearts and minds" of a population.

3. Secrecy is an absolute. In *any* military endeavor, "loose lips sink ships". Therefore, paramilitary operations must represent the pantheon of secrecy. The lengthy chain of command between conventional foot soldiers and their general staff remains so enormous that classified information is guaranteed to reach the press, public, or, especially, the enemy. Paramilitary operations must *always* function covertly; that is, as true "ghosts" on the field.

4. Innovation is the key to success. If conventional – or even "special" – military forces were efficient, there would be no reason for paramilitary forces to exist. A nation could, simply, win its debates through the reputation of being stronger and more *willing* to destroy its enemies. Sadly, conventional militaries remain notoriously inadequate for most of the world's trouble spots. Therefore, paramilitary forces, by definition, must avail themselves of those tactics and equipment ignored by their traditional brethren.

Focusing upon these four elements, paramilitary operations, especially covert ones, become "smaller, cheaper, faster" and far more efficient.

The same holds true for equipment and personnel. Lethality, scheduling, secrecy, and innovation all bespeak of the requirement for functional equipment (and, especially, weapons) and intelligent, common sense-oriented soldiers. War upon the periphery requires that its participants move within the shadows of an apparitional world, guiding its members through the darkest and deepest recesses of combat without sacrificing its warriors to politics, semantics, or tyranny.

## Summary

Wars are often loud, disruptive actions undertaken by standing militaries whose political overseers salivate over how best to kowtow their adversaries into submission through basic posturing. Covert paramilitary operations, to the contrary, offer martial application, plausible deniability, and compartmentalization to clients that seek to control or, at least, dilute the effectiveness of adversarial organizations. These operations serve a set pattern of goals and objectives with their means dictated solely by that particular end. To succeed, however, requires the paramilitary operation to address key requisites of lethality, time, secrecy, and innovation as the focus of martial discipline.

# CHAPTER FOUR:
ON ASYMMETRICAL WARFARE.

NO ONE CAN expect to win full-blown nuclear war with paramilitary forces any more than law enforcement agencies can expect to defeat drug trafficking organizations (DTO) solely with "beat cops" and 9mm pistols. Success in conflict requires an intuitive understanding of *what* the threat represents and *who* best can fight that threat. This does not mean that paramilitary forces may not position themselves to defeat, say, nuclear terrorists or that a police officer may not gather sufficient intelligence to lead to a reduction in that DTO's local capabilities. Rather, fully *understanding* warfare is rarely the specialty of those committed to fighting it.

Despite the relative specialization of soldiering, wars represent a basic human condition if not an outright necessity. It is at the core of the human mind, this inherent nature to fight to survive and to compete against outsiders. Whatever the apparent similarity, however, unless two parties remain evenly matched – inconceivable due to the diversity of the human species – *any* conflict becomes asymmetrical through practice. Even if one were to engage another with precisely the same physical dimensions and attributes, each individual's mindset would have been developed through fundamentally different experiences, fears, anxieties, associations, and hatreds. Regardless of the best efforts enforced – legislatively or culturally – by the politically correct crowd, people *are fundamentally different*. So, too, are their personalities.

Gender reconstruction surgery and social justice, for example, *cannot* fully transform a male into a female or a female into a male. Genetic code remains too complex for that. Nor can a diminutive person expect to win a bout with a heavyweight prize fighter. And, again, an analytical personality may not best a creative individual within the arts even if he or she dominates mathematics. Perhaps more than any other living species, human beings remain truly *asymmetrical* in nature.

The public may truly appreciate this by watching a football or baseball game. Rarely, if ever (even during championships), are both teams evenly matched in strength, talent, health, capability, and record. One side may excel in defense whereas the other may reign with offense. *Something* each side possesses is superior to its opponent and the coach or manager will seek to capitalize on this advantage. This is the hallmark of asymmetrical warfare; to pair one's strengths against another's weaknesses and to alleviate weaknesses against an adversary's strengths. From this perspective, asymmetrical battle is truly a "thinking man's" conflict, one where intelligence reigns supreme.

Covert paramilitary warfare must found itself upon this asymmetrical paradigm if it is to succeed. In as much as openness may lead to disadvantages in secrecy, controlling paramilitary forces through conventional bureaucracy will certainly doom troops through attempts at enforced symmetry. In other words, by destroying asymmetrical natures, you destroy paramilitary functions. The very nature of such asymmetrical warfare rests upon the attributes of mobility, intelligence, initiative, and resolve. We must now discuss these separately so that the student and practitioner of paramilitary forces may better understand their primacy and how best to employ them within his or her unique requirements.

## Maneuver Warfare

Maneuver warfare, it has been defined, represents more than just "moving in relation to the enemy to gain positional advantage" but further "to moving faster than the enemy, to defeating him through superior tempo."[11] By moving faster – physically and mentally – than your enemy, you can keep the asymmetrical equation growing. Stagnation represents the very fabric of bureaucracy and such bureaucracy is what paramilitary forces *should* be seeking to avoid.

As with the aforementioned example involving sports, *motion* is what keeps opponent football teams guessing and, in the case of baseball, both the pitcher and the batter seek to place the ball into a favorable *location* to disrupt the opposition. Player alignments in both sports attempt to sway the adversary into changing *their* positions in a strange minuet of calls and positional shifts designed as much for confusion as functionality. On the battlefield, maneuver *prevents* targeting.

Conventional warfare represents an oversized chess match with its strategic locations, orders of battle, and proudly adorned hierarchy. Despite the introduction of mechanization and air support, little has changed from the days of Napoleonic lines and colorful semaphores. Navies appear to be the worst offenders: ships are numbered and named according to specific vessel class, sailors' uniformed corresponding to specific ranks, and fleets designated according to specific homeports. In conventional militaries, *expectation* becomes cornerstone.

Paramilitary units, in contrast, remain necessarily limited in personnel, equipment, support, and association.

---

[11] Lind, William S. "The Theory and Practice of Maneuver Warfare" in ed. Richard D. Hooker, Jr. *Maneuver Warfare: An Anthology* (Novato, CA: Presidio Press, 1993), 4.

They bear fewer troops than most segments of the conventional army, receive equipment and weapons on an ad hoc basis, suffer support through the whims of political leaders, and are viewed as outcasts by everyone even from within their own ranks. They are truly the bastards of the military world.

For all their problems and troubles, however, paramilitary units prevail through their *mobility* and responsiveness. Smaller, quicker, and (if probably trained) deadlier than their conventional brethren, paramilitary forces epitomize both maneuver and asymmetrical warfare. They can target when opportunity arises, relocate when threats appear, and move *with* their environment rather than simply moving through it. Nevertheless, an intimate understanding of maneuver warfare must still be fused within their existence.

A boxer shackled into a corner is doomed and chess pieces bound to the idiosyncrasies of a player's talent are little more than pawns en masse. Only by breaking the shackles can a fighter hope to recover and the rules of chess are inadequate for lawless combat. Through "freedom" of movement can either hope to achieve some measure of survival within an otherwise uncontrollable situation. Such represents the essence of maneuver warfare (semantics not withstanding).

Because of their limitations, paramilitary forces *must* remain agile and unpredictable. When combined with a covert nature – "movement" by way of deceit and deception, if you will – these smaller units can bedazzle larger, more conventional forces. By engaging within the apparitional theater, paramilitary forces can use their advantages to confuse more restrictive organizations that cannot adapt as quickly or as confidently.

To ensure both effectiveness *and* mobility, paramilitary

forces must restrict themselves to the following activities:

✓ *Raids and ambushes.* Traditionally speaking, both raids and ambushes represent maneuvers, one more active and the other a bit passive. For our discussion, however, we shall define a *raid* as a venture into an environment to attack an enemy unit and an *ambush* as an attack against an adversary entering into an environment. Both imply movement following the attack. Paramilitary units operating within a covert nature offer tremendous advantages in either a raid or an ambush capacity. They are equipped for quick insertion and egress, primed for combat due to the selective nature of its personnel, and bear little of the forewarning that taint bureaucratic, conventional units.

✓ *Intelligence, Surveillance, and Reconnaissance (ISR).* An ability to scout, patrol, and break away from adversarial forces means that paramilitary units can be used most effectively within an ISR function. Their small size, dependence upon local sources for food and shelter, and clandestine nature permit them to gather intelligence about enemy units of nearly any size. Mobility grants them an opportunity to quickly change locations for advantage or disappear into the bush should chance discovery appear.

✓ *Demolitions.* Successful destruction of enemy assets requires an ability to move unnoticed through varied terrain. Secrecy of mission is also of paramount importance for both keeping the target unaware of the pending action and for shielding the demolition team following the strike. Deeper, harder to reach targets also require great mobility in that destruction may have to involve different locations than what were, perhaps, advised during pre-mission intelligence briefings. Paramilitary units bear such ability to change on the fly to ensure success within a host of activities.

Any mission that necessitates quick maneuvering combined with lethal force represents the apex of paramilitary doctrine and this should grant leadership and practitioners advantage over all but the most tyrannical of adversarial forces.

## Actionable Intelligence

For matters of discussion, *intelligence* is referred to that information that may be employed to gain tactical and strategic advantage over an enemy or adversarial forces whether that opponent remains an active belligerent, a hostile governmental agency, or an economic competitor (friendly or not). We will further restrict that intelligence to that which is collected by *human* (HUMINT), *communication* (COMINT), and *geospatial* (GEOINT) assets. Finally, we have listed these assets in order of flexibility; in other words, HUMINT remains more flowing in nature, COMINT a bit more stationary, and GEOINT probably most fixed of all.

Intelligence is key to *any* successful endeavor, for to "know thy enemy" (or any opponent) is tantamount to survival. Operating within hostile environments and/or against hostile forces, one needs as much information about the adversary as possible. Paramilitary units – as with any small, decentralized group – provide the best platform for gaining this actionable intelligence. Their low signature along with flexible mobility permit paramilitary units to melt into local communities as well as shadow opposing forces. Nevertheless, to remain efficient and productive, the specific types of data acquired by paramilitary units – especially covert ones – should be limited.

- ✓ *Environmental.* By this, we mean, the paramilitary unit must obtain information regarding the community, geography, climate, and economy of its area of operation. Functioning within any 4GW requires military forces to protect indigenous populations inasmuch as defeating enemy personnel. This means that each specific community must be properly analyzed for *its* problems and solutions. For example, drug producing locations would require, perhaps, more economic diversity than open counternarcotic battles. The same holds true for urban settings frequented by terrorists. This intelligence provides the *who* and *why* of any conflicts within a given area. Paramilitary units require this information to differentiate citizens from true belligerents and target only those adversaries who cannot be reasoned with.

- ✓ *Historical.* This information includes not only cultural data but pairs that data with historical trends to provide a wide analysis of *what* and *how* things arrived at their current status. For example, what events occurred that keep local citizens from trusting governments or how have foreign interventions magnified this distrust of outsiders. If environmental intelligence provides the snapshot of any present community, then historical intelligence provides the lens through which that image is developed. It provides military forces – and not just paramilitary ones – with exposure to those problems and anxieties that affect the way that local populations think.

✓ *Targeting.* Paramilitary forces, through their function, will bear two targets to consider, one martially and the other in servitude. In the first case, the target will involve adversarial groups and individuals that may need to be neutralized or otherwise compromised. The second case involves the local citizens and civic leaders that should be utilized to accomplish the paramilitary unit's mission. Both considerations must be simultaneous. For example, the targeting of a local (and much despised) despot may remove an enemy and endear the local citizenry at the same time. Targeting intelligence represents that which permits the paramilitary team to better handle its specific missions and may change periodically.

Intelligence, to remain valid, must continue through all aspects of a mission, including pre-mission planning and post-mission debriefing. In this regard, *all* members of the unit become active sensors, each absorbing all that he or she observes, hears, and feels and applying that knowledge to the task at hand.

## Initiative

The primary curse of Westernized militaries remains the relative absence of personal initiative. This further holds true for the hemisphere's corporate environment where micromanagement has seeped into all aspects of the economy. No longer are soldiers (or workers) permitted to adapt to local conditions or envision future needs without endless delays and red tape orchestrated from absentee strategic leadership. That many modernized armies suggest that today's techno-centric forces, armed with networked communications, receive "real-time" instructions from command do not change this at all. Simply put, most soldiers from the West remain enslaved to the doctrinal systems developed through the legislative process.

This problem is also exemplified through Western educational systems that indoctrinate more than teach, leaving students ill-prepared to deal with real-life situations involving controversy and aggression – staples within the asymmetrical battlefield. Accordingly, few individuals are adequately prepared to deal with life or death crises. They haven't been exposed to martial situations in the manner that those in, say, Latin America or Asia experience. Nevertheless, there *are* individuals that fill the need despite bureaucracy's best attempts to corral independent thought.

These individuals do not care for either convention or what elitists consider "rational" thought; they are the renegades, the rebels, the innovators, and, ironically, the *traditionalists* within society (as civilization has traditionally been the proving ground for his or her thoughts). These are individuals brought up to value tinkering, hunting, exploring, experimenting, and may seem a bit quirky to others. Before the videogame age, these individuals learned how to track wildlife, build improvised weaponry (before it became terroristic just to consider), and experiment with chemistry sets (before that became labeled narco-specific). In short, these rare individuals set the pattern of human development before that development became everything but *human* in appreciation.

Fortunately, such individuals *still* exist within society – everywhere – they just have been subdued by the expectations of both liberal progressivism and videogame-centric marketing. To locate such people today, all that is required is to discover their basic personality traits and familial heritage. These attributes may include the following characteristics.

✓ *Monotheism.* In secularized society, religion has become rather taboo. Nevertheless, religious faith does not squash creative thought – it inspires it. Some of the greatest achievements in human history came by way of religion and, in particular, one religious view: monotheism. Those who believe within a singular, *omnipotent* God who created the entire universe share three extremely important considerations: the intrinsic value of human life, the extraordinary beauty of the natural world, and an individual's gravest duty to both explore and protect the prior two subjects. These beliefs allow individuals an opportunity to push his or her mental boundaries beyond the observable (that which is, say, solely taught within public schools) and reconsider imposing rules and regulations offered by society itself.

✓ *Restlessness.* Here, we are *not* discussing reactive personalities nor those with psychoses that promote wanton destruction. Rather, we are considering individuals who cannot hold to the status quo without attempting to make some modifications or propose changes for improvement. In other words, people that do like to tinker a bit to fashion a "better mousetrap" or climb unscalable mountains simply because "they are there". As with physicists and engineers, they enjoy taking things apart just to see how they work and whether he or she can place them back together without instruction.

✓ *Sibling segregation.* This characteristic is functionally specific. What you are looking for are individuals hailing from larger families with some degree of separation between the births of siblings. Born into large families (four or more children) permits the individual to acclimate him or herself to society whereas a few years between births instills the sense of competition and survival that fosters independent thought. Smaller families tend to create people who "cling" to others while closer siblings foster bondage with like-minded individuals.

Although not necessarily an all-inclusive list, these personal characteristics can lead paramilitary leaders towards those individuals most likely to facilitate his or her unit and its subsequent operations.

## Uncompromising Resolve

Due to the nature of paramilitary activity, seeing missions through to the end remains a fundamental goal for unit cohesiveness. Again, Western-style militaries often neglect sufficient training and experience to foster mission objectives amongst their ranks. At best, these armies seek quick and easy "wars" before public appreciation tanks. At worst, their national leaders push the brakes and instigate yet another undeclared conflict that teeters between strictly law enforcement (such as countering narcotics) operations and military counterinsurgency (say, the War against Terror) roles.

We can blame society for this problem as well, for most citizens bear insufficient resolve to handle any crisis more aggravating than paying the utility bill. The conveniences of modern society no longer provide a way of life based upon gut determination, resiliency, and discipline. Even our Big Box retailers are moving into the realm of online grocery pickup and personal shoppers – attesting to the fact that consumers no longer need to actually "shop" for their products outside the toils of manhandling the laptop computer or smart phone.

When "others" now select our toilet paper and toothpaste because we have become too burdened to shop for ourselves, it remains incredulous to believe that *we* may have to end our wars during our tenure as national leader or, alternatively, that *we citizens* may have to make sacrifices to ensure our own survival. With a loss of accountability, we lose our momentum for enduring any crisis that may require shattering the status quo of our existence. In this regard, the more convenience-laden we become, the less likely we are to produce true warriors.

Paramilitary operations, sadly, require warriors in the truest definition of the word. More so than, perhaps, even our illustrious special operations soldiers who, though remarkably adaptable, still remain fixed upon conventional army discipline and logistics. Paramilitaries shatter the expectations of specialty and reward combat with genuine primal ordinariness. These individuals do not enact militarism with the simply donning of a uniform; they are, and will always be, soldiers whenever their heart beats.

In the past, paramilitary soldiers had always been conscripted into service, either through guerrilla indoctrination or political shenanigans. These individuals, at best, simply came from the "resigned guerrilla" camp.[12] They were thrust into a conflict for which he or she held no desire to serve and acquiesced to the notion that any chance of staying alive was to serve the cause until he or she could affect an escape. That desire to leave the mission explains why they are not necessarily decent paramilitaries to recruit in the first place.

---

[12] Godlewski, R.J. *Practical Guerrilla Warfare* (Charleston, SC: CreateSpace Independent Publishing Platform, 2015), 28.

Modern paramilitaries need to be a bit more disciplined and resolved within his or her attention to conflict. Success must be based upon survival and victory, not simply escape from the conflict. Countless civilian populations have survived and escaped from massive conflicts, yet we would not immediately characterize them as bona fide warriors (even if most understand the horrors of war better than Western special operators). Survival implies victory and victory means winning.

Inasmuch as any aircraft landing that you can walk away from is a good thing, any battle that you can *walk* away from is a good fight. In this context, walking – as opposed to, say, running haphazardly – implies a conscious control of one's motions, direction, and security. Even within retreat, this means that the soldier fully understands his situation and condition, taking into full account the environment and perceivable threats. In other words, full coordination of one's senses and options.

Conscript soldiers generally do not possess such self-awareness, nor are they adequately trained to heighten such senses. These conspire to forestall any initiative or resolve in solving crises – whether martial, operational, or personal. The individual, without such abilities, rapidly loses confidence within his or her capability to function within alien environments. They became tame at best and dysfunctional at worst. These attributes seriously undermine paramilitary operations – let alone covert ones.

To succeed, paramilitary soldiers *must* resolve to carry out his or her function with the greatest efficiency, dedication, and professionalism. Anything less than this permits the soldier to become complacent – even negligent – and the organization parasitical. By this, we mean, that nonprofessional paramilitary groups descend into abject radicalism and soldiers become thugs at best and terrorists at worst. Misled and ill-conceived forces dominate the planet and offer populations (and the media) with sufficient reason to join the "other side" whomever that may represent.

Dilution of capability, whether mentally or operationally, leads paramilitary forces to dissolve into mere "irregulars", perhaps the best developed term for those forces without organization. Covert paramilitary operations, in contrast, focus upon the need for secrecy and the application of martial military efforts upon an unsuspecting enemy. This necessitates a need for sound discipline and actionability, components that can only be substantiated through effective training and utilization.

## Summary

The essence of warfare rests with the asymmetrical conflicts that govern its battlefield and participants. Contrary to popular opinion, however, *all* martial conflicts involve the asymmetrical equation as war remains as diverse as the humanity that staffs it. Success within these myriad of asymmetrical conflicts requires mobility, intelligence, initiative, and resolve amongst its participants. In this regard, maneuver warfare, actionable intelligence, command initiative, and personal resolve remain hallmark for victory. In turn, these conditions require innovative and resolute individuals.

# CHAPTER FIVE:
PRACTICAL TRAINING OF PARAMILITARIES.

TO VENTURE INTO battle with novices represents a major miscalculation on the part of military and organizational leadership, whether that group represents a strong national sovereignty or simply a loose network of likeminded rebels. As humanity's most primal activity, martial conflict requires the most capable of individuals and the best training available. Sadly, even within major standing armies, these requisites are neglected for both political and economic reasons. In the first case, few leaders desire to foster a group of actual *warriors*. In the second case, efficient militaries are not inherently expensive, which diminishes the returns on investment for those endeared to the "military industrial complex".

A major obstacle towards training of paramilitary forces deals with the quality and quantity of the available recruitment pool. Too often, particularly amongst Third World regional groups, individuals are conscripted from seminally hostile communities or accepted from overzealous parties that seek to adjust the mission towards his or her most desirous cause. In either case, the paramilitary group suffers from amateur soldiers that individually decide when and where they shall adhere to the mission at hand.

These part-time soldiers are a menace regardless of whether they occupy friendly or enemy camps as they represent little more than opportunists functioning within a mole capacity. Because they cannot be corralled for any length of time, their presence represents a "wildcard" upon the battlefield and within operational plans. Accordingly, great care must be taken to ensure that *only those individuals* that meet the expectations of strategic and tactical objectives are sought and recruited.

Selection efforts must be made through consideration of the personality, mental frame of mind, culture, and maturity of the target recruits. From here, the group seeking such individuals can gauge whether or not the person under review bears sufficient intelligence, education, foresight, and adaptability to be welcomed into the martial organization. Those promising candidates that lack some of these attributes can be absorbed into less demanding, non-combat roles that could free others for martial engagements. Regardless, extreme care should be taken to ensure that none of the recruits deceive paramilitary leaders; honesty is more important than anything else, for upon this foundation an individual bases his or her entire life (and don't be fooled – *everyone* fibs at one point or another).

## Square One: The Recruit

The most accomplished warrior in history begins life as a raw recruit. From Joan of Arc on through Audie Murphy and today's unknown "super soldiers", *everyone* hails from immaturity and family restrictions. That some grow up faster than others does not change that reality. A "kid" in Africa or Latin American, for instance, may become just as lethal as a veteran from the United States or Europe. In fact, some of history's greatest warriors *were* children by today's standards (e.g., Alexander the Great, Joan of Arc, etc.). Nevertheless, these should be considered exceptions to the rule for modernity requires that paramilitary forces avoid traumatizing children at all costs.

Despite this handicap, there remain a great many individuals that fit the need for martial combat and would be willing to fight for the cause if so properly motivated by that group's leadership. If, therefore, age is restricted, then the following characteristics should be examined.

**Table 1. Desired attributes of Paramilitary Recruit.**

|  | Not desirable | Desirable | Most Desirable |
|---|---|---|---|
| **Maturity** | Truancy and aggression. | Well balanced and behaved. | Sound mixture of heritage and personal experience. |
| **Independence** | Individualism and introversion. | Independent thought and expression. | Personal contribution towards doctrine. |
| **Explorative** | Techno-centricity as a crutch. | Outdoorsmanship. | Outdoorsmanship with technology as a tool. |
| **Craftsmanship** | Lack of resourcefulness. | Ability to fabricate. | True innovator. |
| **"Knowledge Curator"** | Lack of memory. | Substantial memory. | Able to catalog and recall effortlessly. |

In Table 1 we can observe the most desirable traits for recruits, for which we shall now elaborate.

From the table, we can see that the most desirous individual to recruit represents one whose maturity rests upon a solid mixture of upbringing and empirical knowledge, whose independence establishes a basis for doctrinal addition, an outdoorsman who merely uses technology for a tool rather than as a crutch, innovates by way of habit, and can catalog and recall information gained rather effortlessly. Of course, such an individual is exceedingly rare within *any* community. Nevertheless, these remain reputable goals to seek.

Time and effort should focus on recruiting individuals that bear a suitable mixture of these qualities and locate him or her within an operation that best utilizes what each has to offer. For instance, most properly reared individuals fall within that segment of maturity that borders "behaved" and that which expresses experience mixed with adherence towards culture and upbringing. As maturation remains an evolving process, these individuals *will* progress towards that most desirous aspect of completely fusing tradition and discovery. Conversely, however, an individual whose maturity is not as desirable – that of one who frequently flaunts duties and exhibits unprovoked aggression – likely will *not* mature sufficiently to enter a well-balanced mentality.

Similarly, an individual who lacks comparable memory will *not* evolve into a "knowledge curator"; a person able to draw upon a wealth of knowledge acquired through experience and education. He or she will simply not be able to remember enough details to guide his or her future actions without external guidance. Therefore, a keen memory and the ability to decipher knowledge for effect remains an exceedingly valuable trait of successful paramilitary personnel. This type of individual will further rely more upon personal inquisitiveness – the "explorative" aspect of life – than technology to succeed.

The paramilitary commander or recruiter will have to determine which of these traits best apply to their unique situation with acquiring as many of the "most desirable" traits as possible knowing that, at a minimum, the desirables will evolve with time. Each individual will be carefully vetted to foster a soldier eager to learn, able to behave in the field, and knowledgeable enough to learn and teach others about what he or she learns through experiences in the field. The raw recruit, then, becomes a profitable soldier, equivalent to conventional militaries' noncommissioned officers (NCO).

## "Shock Training"

Every soldier on the planet began life as a civilian, even those born and bred into prestigious military families. No one intuitively knows how to handle a firearm, camouflage themselves in the bush, stalk prey, and, most especially, kill an opponent. The process by which bright-eyed pupils emerged as steely, throat-slitting professionals has been best described as total immersion, "shock training" by others.[13] It is a process so brief and in-depth as to literally shatter that recruit's familial upbringing and social slushiness. This shock transforms citizens into warriors.

For paramilitary value, such training must include:

1. *Total physical transformation.* War represents an endurance battle, one whose stakes are literally life and death. Traditionally, soldiers have ranged from seemingly steroid abusers on one end through blatantly obese on the other. Both stereotypes suggest a complete lack of physical conditioning and discipline amongst the military ranks. Yet, paramilitary conflicts should not be driven into the attritional camp through lack of individual conditioning. Rather, paramilitary soldiers should remain more agile than either obese or "gym queen" examples and better match those frontiersmen that served American expansion during the eighteenth and nineteenth centuries well. These pioneers were able to run for days, handle the chores of living in the forest well, and administer to a great many personal injuries. And not a single one of these individuals lifted weights as a hobby.

---

[13] Balor, Paul. *Manual of the Mercenary Soldier* (Boulder: Paladin Press, 1988), 83-85.

2. *Weapons proficiency.* Both standing armies and conscripted local varieties leave much to be desired when it comes to firearm and ammunition utilization. During wars – American Civil War, World War I, World War II, etc. – a great many soldiers had repeatedly failed to fire their weapons at the enemy despite consciously appearing to do so.[14] A Congressional study following U.S. engagement in Vietnam showed that an average of 50,000 rounds were fired by American soldiers to inflict a single casualty. Research has conclusively proven that *most people* simply cannot shoot another human being (even if 65% of the human population can inflict lethality upon an innocent victim through simple authoritative "peer pressure"[15]). To counter this discrepancy in both firing ability and ammunition waste, a fundamental and substantial amount of the recruit's time should be spent on the shooting range with realistic targets that move and mimic the way that actual people do when shot (improvisation can overcome technical challenges here).

3. *Fieldcraft.* Being in top physical shape and knowing how to place a round dead center from a thousand meters away does not constitute representing a soldier, good over otherwise, as many Hollywood actors remain in top condition and several Olympic sports entail accurate shooting (some require being even in better shape). What separates soldiers from actors and sporting enthusiasts involves survival upon the battlefield and herein is where the

---

[14] Grossman, *On Killing*, 23-29.
[15] Ibid, 141-143.

warrior confronts both enemy *and* nature. To function well, soldiers must be able to live off the land, construct survivable shelters, heal a myriad of wounds and injuries, and move without disrupting the environment or being observed by technology. In this regard, the Selous Scouts of the former Rhodesia sent raw recruits into the wild for a couple of weeks *prior* to launching them into a training program. This Gideonesque task certainly culled the ranks of potential recruits, offering survivors a chance to truly utilize the new knowledge they gained from others. Paramilitary recruits, necessitating a complete lifestyle away from conveniences, must learn to forage for food and literally meld into the environment to escape attention. Therefore, it remains best to select from those who have already proven that they can survive without anything given to them.

4. *Competitive adaptation.* People tend to learn from both abstract technical (*Techne*) and experiential, intuitive (*Mētis*) knowledge.[16] This knowledge is further achieved through competitive adaptation gained from rival sources.[17]Inasmuch as terrorist and trafficking organizations can improvise from adversarial experiences for their own benefit, paramilitary groups must also employ that which works from enemy groups as well. A brilliant idea is, after all, a brilliant idea no matter *who* has invented the technique. In this regard, paramilitary recruits must first be free to

---

[16] Michael Kenney *From Pablo to Osama: Trafficking and Terrorist Networks, Government Bureaucracies, and Competitive Adaptation* (University Park: The Pennsylvania State University Press, 2008), 4.
[17] Ibid., 6-7.

experiment and discover new methods to ageless problems without the cumbersome burden of following established doctrine to the letter. In the field of battle, *winning* remains the only strategy to endorse even if 'winning' means retreating in order to fight another day. Any group that a paramilitary force will be confronting has likely been required to experience the same shortages of time, personnel, and resources. What they learned already could save precious time discovering anew. Efforts must be made to ensure that such learning is promoted and not stifled; recruits must be rewarded if he or she can best established doctrine.

These characteristics permit the individual to grow from tunnel-vision civilian into an all-aware warrior, but they are, in themselves, not particularly valuable without further nurturing the mindset. The sharpened recruit must undergo further training to refine the martial instincts so necessary in conflict.

## The Technical Warrior

Not too long ago, the U.S. Army had been paying out $2,000 daily per student to have its soldiers become proficient in Kalashnikov firearms. That the U.S. had active soldiers unfamiliar with the most popular rifle in history and paid more than double what the firearm – and several hundred rounds of ammunition – would cost to purchase on a *daily basis* to instruct its warriors remains a staple of Western military idiocy. Such bureaucracies can never win wars; they merely manage them until their citizens forget what they were fighting for.

The other problem that bureaucratic, conventional armies thrust upon their ranks involves the adage that larger, more technologically sophisticated (and costly) weapons are better than those that simply kill one-on-one. Wars are very destructive, they seem to think, so a few hundred more innocent casualties here or there will not make much of a difference in the grander scheme of things. That is, until these armies have to fight again within that particular region and find few allies willing to cooperate.

Technology, properly used as a tool and not as a crutch, can reduce the number of persons that need to be killed *and* shorten the time required for aggressors to be active within the region. It is a simple matter of shoot the adversary, inspire the locals, perhaps smile to the children, and then beeline for the border. In military speak, it means going in and doing the job and then retreating home before *anyone* cares that you are there. Promoting the deployment of thousands of soldiers but saying that you expect to leave the invaded country "by Christmas time" has soured a great many conflicts throughout the centuries. Unfortunately, paramilitary forces – and, especially, covert ones – do not possess the luxury of telegraphing their movements or intentions.

Such apparitional forces need to rely upon technology to reduce their signature. They need advanced communications to coordinate team members, to position their forces surgically, and to extract themselves from the location without raising suspicions that they were ever *there*. In comparison, conventional forces parade in front of the media, insert (usually) by helicopter, and board large, commercial transports for the trip home. In a sense, their operation *in situ* represents only a third of the time shown to the public; the remaining theatrics involving deployment and return – very much openly, and very much *political.*

Once individual paramilitary soldiers have been

trained on how to live off the land, fieldstrip any number of weapons blinded folded (and with live fire exercises going on around him or her), camouflage hides so that even their instructors cannot locate them, and administer first aid to all but the most horrendous of injuries, only *then* can we introduce them to such technology as night vision, micro communications, global positioning satellite (GPS) systems, and similar technologies.

In view of Murphy's Law that states that anything that can go wrong will and at the worst conceivable time, soldiers must be trained to function *without* the technology that Western armies cling to. Reading maps, for instance, has been a time-honored skill that has saved countless lives over the course of the centuries, but until a soldier knows how to visualize that terrain within his or her mind, reading that map will prove useless in the end. One must ensure that technology (the map in this example) can soundly mesh with primal experiences so that the soldier can *confirm* that the highest peak, say, represented on the map is not dwarfed by three others that the eye detects.

Every piece of technology, from handheld maps on through stealth bombers rests upon the laurels of *human* craftsmen and scientists; errors are frequent amongst that which comes artificially. For this reason alone, technology must, again, exist as a servant and not a master, for its presence is often affected by electricity, climatic conditions, and misuse – attributes that the human body has learned to bypass through millions of years of evolution.

To forestall any problems, paramilitary students must progress through his or her training in distinct segments depending upon the technology available. For example, if one were teaching a group how to maneuver through the environment, such a process might look like the following:

1. *Geographical Awareness*. Student recruits are

introduced to the physical and geological terms and conditions of his or her environment. They are taught the peculiarities, say, of different rivers and mountains, which trees grow where and when, and which animals are likely to appear during specific times of the day and year. Most importantly, they are shown how these features and wildlife would appear both during daytime and at night. Only when students can properly identify these features will they be introduced to the next step.

2. *Map Reading.* Once they can adequately observe and identify what exists in nature, students are introduced to map reading and learn how to fix all the "two-dimensional" icons of the map upon their "three-dimensional" memories and past observations. For example, without more than the elevation lines of the map, they are assigned the task of correlating those drawings to a certain number of mountains that they may have seen photographs of but had not previously seen. This will get them to analyze the printed and "real" representations of geospatial information.

3. *Tracking.* Sufficiently trained in both observation and map reading, the students' next assignment would be to track an instructor through a given area with only a few maps available to guide the students along. This would not be a "tracking" exercise, per se, but simply one that forces them to rely upon maps and human observation as they are led through a "foreign" environment previously unknown to them. Following the instructor simply pulls them into a distant location from which the group must find their way back from with only

a brief map by which to guide him or her.

4. *GPS.* Proficient in the field, students are turned towards the wonders (and shortcomings) of satellite navigation. These exercises should serve two distinct functions: one in which the students are challenged to determine the veracity of the equipment and the second in how to respond should that equipment fail. The initial exercises should allow the students to confirm that the GPS equipment is providing their location as, hopefully, more accurate and timelier than what they perceive from the map. Follow-up exercises should be undertaken with faulty equipment (e.g., poorly charged batteries, etc.) that are guaranteed to fail at unpredictable times. This forces the student to question *what* their equipment is telling them and whether they can learn of these shortcomings quickly enough to avert any number of situations that the astute instructor may force upon the group.

Technology is great *when* it works, so paramilitary soldiers must be trained to employ the equipment when available but not waste precious time focusing upon its merits.

## Summary

Paramilitary recruits must go through total immersion "shock training" to transform them into native warriors, able to venture into hostile terrain without fear. Only when he or she is able to literally "live off the land" will they be able to avail him or herself to the wealth of technology that modern society permits the covert warrior some degree of convenience.

# CHAPTER SIX:
COVERT PARAMILITARY OPPORTUNITIES.

PARAMILITARY OPERATIONS SHOULD not be arbitrarily confused with guerrilla operations, for both bear peculiarities that may distinguish one from the other. For example, guerrilla operations may arise out of necessity, for the authoring force bears few personnel and supports to support a full-scale military assault against an adversary. In contrast, paramilitary operations, generally defined, remain *planned* operations, which means that the entity organizing and planning them *may* possess sufficient conventional forces but desires to withhold accountability from. This latter attribute introduces the very concept of *covertness* within the equation.

Furthermore, most guerrilla forces remain "official" if only in the capacity that their leaders encourage devotion to the cause or hostility towards adversaries. Whether loyal to leftist, say, or narcotics trafficking organizations, *true* guerrilla forces do not shy away from their presence as would someone promoting assassination or kidnapping. In this latter regard, paramilitary forces may employ strictly civilians operating within a "military-like" role for pure convenience, but their function, though possessing *military bearing*, is not necessarily military in function.

For matters of this discussion, we can suggest several opportunities for paramilitary operations, particularly those of a covert nature, that do not fundamentally require a 'rank and file' military organization. Instead, we shall assume that these operations parallel that of true military maneuvers solely through their use of firearms, application of violence, and dedicated training. In the use of firearms, we shall include all those tactical and/or logistical arrangements that permit the group to attack or defend itself martially. Violence, in this regard, refers simply to the *intensity* of any particular action, and training underscores a fundamental commitment towards excellence.

## Operations within Ungoverned Spaces

A major, international concern amongst established nations remains the concept of "ungoverned spaces" – colloquially defined as those places where rule of law seems out of place at best or non-existent at worst. While it is noted herein that very few – if any – actual locations exist outside some form of governance, we shall retreat to the same considerations of equating "alternate government" with lack of electoral or tyrannical rule. That is, we shall define our interpretation of ungoverned spaces as:

- ✓ Territories where laws are neither enacted by legislatures nor written for all residents to ponder;

- ✓ Social mechanisms for enforcing this rule of law arise outside national or public referendum (i.e., any policing is left to opportunists);

- ✓ The boundaries for the territory in question remain indeterminable or shifting, with no focus upon specific zones of enforcement;

- ✓ The territory under analysis remains more exclusionary than inclusive (e.g., vehemently

> hostile to outsiders with no personal acceptance of the conditions for which immigration is permitted);

✓ Areas not universally recognized by the broader community of nations.

In these conditions, we risk exposing ourselves to a range of exceptions, but for matters of discussion we shall forfeit debate and focus upon these trends. Nor shall we assume that such "ungoverned spaces" cannot coexist within some very recognized sovereignties (e.g., some areas in Paris where French police avoid).

That we cannot adequately define such locations *and* that many others prohibit honest response suggest a prime target for covert paramilitary operations. If an administration, for instance, wanted to quell urban dissent without infuriating the rest of its constituency, then it might unleash a paramilitary operation against that cell under the premise of rival gang activities. In this regard, the covert paramilitary function would not be a "military" or even "law enforcement" response but suggesting another case of street violence run amok. Few within the public, it is argued, would care to distinguish the difference between "ordinary" violence and an extremely well-coordinated brand.

Ungoverned spaces of the style that we are characterizing allow for transition and transformation. On the one hand, any presence of interlopers necessitates a violent and asymmetrical reaction from local enforcers. On the other hand, their very nature suggests a tendency to keep internal affairs from reaching the broader planet. That there is no size requirement – review Chicago in 2018, for reference – further implicates the violence of these regions as the smaller the ungoverned entity, the greater its chances for violent eruption.

The prospects for covert paramilitary operations within ungoverned areas remains paramount, for these represent the kind of locations that official, state-centric actors prefer to employ non-state solutions for convenience. That is, if one were to conduct activities within a region where human survival may be very limited, then it is best to employ those forces that one can deny the very existence of. For many such state-actors (e.g., the United States during the Bay of Pigs fiasco), the rationale for employing paramilitary forces – if not duly covert – rests within their implied "expendable" status: if an organization can dismiss any knowledge of their existence, then it becomes incredulous to even worry about their demise.

For more effective practitioners, however, paramilitary forces offer an opportunity to sway the trends within ungoverned spaces and then act according to the pursuant outcome. It provides the sponsoring entity a chance to change the outcome, or at least minimalize the effects of failure while all the long forfeiting any connection to the effort one way or another.

Most importantly, because paramilitary forces – unlike "conventional" guerrillas – are not bound to the uniformed status of *visible* military forces, they can readily disappear into ungoverned territories without arousing undue attention. That they are covert – and expendable – keeps most sponsors from caring whether or not they violate international norms. In this regard, they remain covert to the very letter of the definition.

Every national leader, local despot, even corporate executive dreams of a group that can lay martial offense upon a competitor or irritant. The first fears disclosure, the second failure, while the third risk. Politicians govern his or her life through the polls. Tyrants, for his (women are somewhat rare in this category) role, merely fear failure in that they may have aggravating the opposition rather than silence it. As for corporate executives, they remain relative cowards at heart and usually pause within his or her ambitions upon the slightest risk to their position.

Nevertheless, as state-sponsored and taxpayer-funded resources diminish amongst an ever-growing population, the presence of so-called ungoverned spaces will likely become the norm rather than the exception. In this capacity, there will only be one of three options available: confront them, ignore them, or hope to avoid them. Globalization and sheer trajectory will eliminate the last option. Social media and instant data communications will make the second equally impractical. The final option – to directly confront these "lawless environments" may shepherd in the notion to fight chaotic fire with extrajudicial flames. In other words, to employ covert paramilitary forces to gain strategic and tactical advantage from within a midst of countering possibilities.

## Anti-Trafficking Operations

During the 21st Century, *trafficking* has morphed into an all-inclusive transnational criminal scourge upon the planet. No longer is the mere smuggling of narcotics, weapons, or human beings the exclusive domain of one criminal enterprise or another. Given the extreme profitability of these vices – and a great deal more through the peripheral – *all* major criminal enterprises will broach these opportunities eventually. The rewards are too great, the relative risks too little.

Understanding the asymmetrical nature of the trafficking threat provides both governments and NGOs with sufficient reason to target these criminal enterprises. That more has not been done to extinguish the threat has more to do with an inability to muster the courage to fight the criminals until utter victory than it does with lacking proper personnel or weaponry. That a great many politicians favor the existence of these organizations – as with, say, those who espouse illegal immigration or "open border" policies – suggests political profiteering than personal adherence. As such, countertrafficking attention is divided between the weak-minded and the politically strong-willed – hardly ever about national or international security.

Nevertheless, covert paramilitary operations offer advantages for both the socially weak and the politically strong. That is, paramilitary operations can help to posture the timid and sharpen the already powerful but hesitant to act. Such activities offer a 'win-win' situation for those whose mind is firm but fueled by a faint heart. At least in theory.

As with all martial functions, hesitancy and dilution represent the death of formal action. To succeed within any endeavor requires total submission, which is why "shock training" represents the basis for individual military training. Half measures lead to quarter results – at best. Paramilitary efforts, more so than conventional military operations, represent a solutional goal rather than a dynamic transformation. Its use foresees a quicker fix to a nagging issue whereas conventional forces may be employed to offset aggression.

Without a sharp reduction in demand, the best way to defeat trafficking operations – especially that involving narcotics – remains to target critical nodes within that organization's network, removing critical suppliers, personnel, transportation hubs, laboratory technicians, etc. Force multiplication mandates that each strike carry the most effective use of power. Because of this, those individuals and facilities that are irreplaceable to the trafficking organization must be targeted first – and hit the hardest. Such application of dynamic power is best served through *professional* paramilitary operations.

In an age when "special" becomes a catchall phrase in military parlance, effective covert paramilitary operations must ensure the highest level of integrity, expertise, training, and personal commitment to succeed. Again, paramilitary forces are *not* necessarily guerrilla forces – amateurism must be avoided at all costs. That most trafficking organizations bear greater finances than comparable governmental institutions underscore this need for excellence.

There can be no better action to take against the trafficking of drugs, weapons, or humans than for some reputable agency or group to deploy small, covert teams that can infiltrate a known criminal hideout, assassinate a few key individuals and then egress to another location outside the prying eyes of governmental watchdogs or obsessive media outlets. While this scenario may seem a bit pretentious to some and (mostly for the 'special' military branches) sacrilegious to others, the trafficking organizations *already do* carry out such functions in reverse. They care less about stepping upon others' toes when it comes to protecting *their* lives and businesses.

## Counterpiracy Deployments

Maritime piracy represents a lucrative, billion-dollar business heralding from an era when even slavery and drug trafficking remained inconceivable. Today, with larger vessels and the implications of maritime terrorism, the hijacking, confiscation, and/or ransoming of ships earns the interests of a vast conglomerate of transnational criminal organizations and international government agencies, all of which swirl within the paramilitary world.

That piracy intrudes upon both the previous categories – ungoverned spaces and trafficking – should not go unnoticed. The hijacking of large cargo vessels, their secreting to clandestine ports, and then, finally, the "recommissioning" of the ship to serve (unknowingly or otherwise) another company serve to dilute the legalities involved within the criminal trade.

Accordingly, sometimes the most effective way to curb criminal activity remains to send in a lethal force to impart martial justice. As piracy maneuvers within that netherworld of legalities and criminality, between sovereignties and thuggery, *covert* paramilitary operations, especially, allow the practitioner to suggest both insecurity and danger for those who seek to profit from commandeering vessels. That most of these vessels are stolen within the Malacca Straits or around the Horn of Africa means that these bastions of criminal activity hail from regions far from the watchful eyes of the voting public of other nations. As such, conventional militaries would not serve well without perceived legitimacy – something few constituents understand unless he or she were directly threatened.

In this regard, paramilitary operations offer an opportunity for maritime irregular warfare (MIW), the littoral *specialization* of amphibious (insertion via helicopter or airplane not practical) forces trained and equipped to flush out pirates and other criminals from unsecured coastlines. They may further modernize the "Q-ship" concept; laying in wait aboard decoy vessels hoping to attract the pirates salivating for a chance at an easy target merely to find the vessel crewed by numerous well-trained and equipped paramilitary commandos.

Because counterpiracy and MIW operations remain far more specific and devotional than, say, colloquial "guerrilla" activities, their specialization far exceeds that of any comparable martial activity. It is not suggested that these personnel be cross-trained for other, less maritime-intensive duties. Nor should they be employed strictly for intelligence-gathering missions benefiting conventional forces;

paramilitary forces must *always* be shielded from the bureaucracies that handcuff militaries. If the covert forces are utilized to gather intelligence, then it must be *only that intelligence* which is needed by that particular group or sister outfits organized by the original practitioner or client.

## Urban Gang Insurrections

Every large – and a great many smaller – city on the planet bears an evolving gang problem. Chicago, Moscow, Tokyo, Rio de Janeiro, Shanghai, and London, just to name a few, suffer from uncontrolled gang violence to varying degrees. Violence within these larger communities often attracts the attention of the international media before turning our attention back towards other, more trivial matters. Smaller communities throughout the world do not necessarily possess the luxury of having a major news outlet nearby, so atrocities within those locations – ever more fueled by drugs such as methamphetamines – go unnoticed by all but those directly affected.

That violence often erupts – and continues – at so many different locations and cultures proves beyond a reasonable doubt that local legislation and law enforcement efforts remain lacking, to say the least. Almost daily on the news can a resident find an example of gang activity from within even the most "peaceful" of communities. That residents in southwestern Iowa should find themselves tucked into human trafficking or those living in western Oklahoma should discover teenage hoodlumism rampant says more about the ignorance of those residents than it does about the rarity of these crimes.

When street violence turns to murder, rape, stabbings, beatings, and other aggressive forms of intimidation, it can only be deemed a full-scale war. When, as in Mexico, severed heads are rolled across crowded dance floors, this "war" becomes yet another atrocity. Multiply these crimes across international boundaries and dismiss local constabularies and these atrocities morph into abject genocide. At some point, concerned officials – or even business and community leaders – must draw the line and *fight* the evil forces invading their cities.

*Covert* paramilitary operations offer an opportunity – though admittedly an extrajudicial one – to take the fight back to the streets and impart "actionable justice" on those groups whose presence perennially evades incarceration. When human lives are at risk, human *action* must rise to the occasion, and it remains perfectly human to defend oneself. So just *how*, it must be argued, can such paramilitary teams affect urban crime without engaging a host of legal issues?

First, it must be argued that *all* covert military or paramilitary operations transcend legality. If they were legit – in the liberal, international sense – then their function would not have to be secretive. Second, "plausible deniability" does not have to be taken within the context of *other's* laws; do not believe for a moment that even within liberal democracies, government agencies do *not* secretly engage their citizens. Third, the victor *always* defines the acceptable rules of engagement, which is why criminals have been getting away with literal murder for decades; the criminals *win* their battles. Finally, very few citizens squawk over the prospects of leading better lives, feeling secure within his or her home, and sending their children to schools without barricades and roving guards.

Nevertheless, productive paramilitary operations within the urban setting warrant extreme prejudice in personnel selection and methods, otherwise the covert group will simply become just another criminal element unleashing indiscriminate violence upon an unsuspecting population. To succeed through "moral law" – if not legislative law – these groups must become exceedingly surgical in operation, something that even "special operators" of the elite military services do not always offer. All groups obtain "pirates" – individuals whose personal actions taint its reputation and lead others astray – but small paramilitary units cannot afford even the slightest hint of impropriety.

Such urban operations bear two "legitimate" purposes. First, to target instigating gang personnel who may be unapproachable to local law enforcement. Here, we are violating the letter of the law by introducing the concept of covert removal – not necessarily killing – of people whose presence unleashes violent crimes upon a particular neighborhood through direct or *directed* actions. By violating the spirit of the law, we acknowledge that such laws remain obstacles to enforcing peace and security within our towns and cities. The use of covert, extrajudicial forces to calm these disturbances simply provides "authority" an easy way out of a troubling situation. That is, by keeping the public (and media) away from the activities at hand, local and private officials may boast of reducing violence through other, more acceptable measures that, frankly, heretofore had been impractical.

The second legitimate application of urban paramilitary forces operating within a covert capacity remains proactive intelligence gathering and surveillance. Most police agencies are hampered by procedural law and state legislation. Sometimes, however, information is required that comes not by way of "chain of custody" or constitutional jurisprudence. In this regard, covert paramilitary personnel may be able to conduct espionage operations unavailable to comparatively ill-trained law enforcement personnel. Furthermore, civic prosecutors may be able to introduce evidence into court if it just "happens" to find its way into his or her office. At a minimum, investigations may be initiated based upon this information *if* its collection is not traceable to the authorities conducting the prosecutorial process.

Paramilitary operations within the urban environment strongly suggest the realization that organized crime within the cities has escalated into a war, a style of conflict beyond the preparations and limitations of traditional police forces and, yet, far away from the inclusion of military units of liberal democracies. The covert use of such forces enforces the attitude that "sometimes" laws have to be violated to protect populations from those whose indifference to any law makes communities uncivilized or as Herman Melville put it, "uncomfortable inns in which to dwell".

## Summary

Covert paramilitary operations, as fully secure and clandestine martial applications, offer many opportunities for their employment. Amongst these include operations within ungoverned spaces, against traffickers and pirates, and within contested urban neighborhoods. Their foundation rests upon the fact that those employing these groups cannot be identified (if the operation remains effective and professional) with their operation. This, of course, implies that such paramilitary operations are inherently extrajudicial and, therefore, outside the legality of democratic societies. Nevertheless, there remain periods when the "good of society" outweighs the "rights" of criminality and herein is where covert paramilitary units operate within the netherworld of morality versus duty.

\

# CHAPTER SEVEN:
## COVERT PARAMILITARY WARFARE.

WITHIN THIS PARTICULAR volume, we have introduced covert paramilitary operations as a clandestine martial function designed to impart violence within closed or otherwise unapproachable scenarios plaguing bureaucracies and threatening communities. That is, paramilitary activities exist as those "military like" solutions where conventional armies and even police forces may be impractical or illegal to employ. To adequately comprehend this surreal world of officialdom versus sanctioned indiscretion, we must retreat a bit and discuss the field through a broader narrative.

Despite the best intentions of society to color events with pastels or orchestrate various levels of monochrome grayness, life remains a distinctly black and white endeavor to behold. Things are either right or wrong, legal or illegal, warranted or not. That laws may be "interpreted" or otherwise diluted does not alter their existence any more than aggression can be silenced away through compassion and consideration.

Into this world of stark realities lays the four prospects that any individual or group considers when it confronts threats: running, surrendering, posturing, or fighting. Most bureaucracies favor the first three. They prefer to run away and divert through legislation, surrender to the challenge and ignore its presence, or posture within the media as if the newest administration or candidate bears an effective solution for the crisis at hand. Only tyrannies tend to prefer to fight and, more often than not, this action equates with using a sledgehammer to drive in a tack.

Problems deserve solutions. Solutions deserve practicality. And practicality deserves efficiency and resolve. Anything less than this progression leads to interminable inadequacy. In other words, by placing bandages upon gaping wounds, officials and other civic leaders merely sponge up the festering effects of the problem rather than cauterizing the nemesis to begin with. In fact, failure to apply adequate "first aid" to *any* crisis represents something of effective job security for those in control of the problem. Never a good idea.

Indecision – or even compromise – never finds results. The literal "civilization shattering" Peloponnesian War – as with the First World War a great many centuries later – began largely because a remote skirmish touched off an intricate web of alliances and counter-alliances throughout the Greek world that attempted to keep such wars from erupting. These machinations to prevent conflict simply – and usually – serve as little but kindling to fuel future conflagrations.

Aside from those conflicts that refuse to hide within history rests several much smaller intrigues that bypass the attention of the public and media. These conflicts range from small urban power struggles on through border disputes, each submerging within the great debate of, say, socialization or immigration. Nevertheless, whenever the power to irreparably harm human lives avails itself, the issue becomes, once again, potentially civilization shattering.

From Bosnia, to Rwanda, to Darfur, for example, the world rests within regions of human conflict that become epitomes for aggression, but often disappear from the public mind over the course of a very brief period of time. Even today (2018), the Nazi Holocaust becomes fodder for deniers and revisionists. These conflicts arise and fade through peoples' incapacity to act. Governments and institutions fear getting involved and then often pass the responsibility towards future generations as they invoke international tribunal after international tribunal.

Even with the advent of social media and the Internet, trafficking, terrorism, drugs, and slavery remain on the rise, suggesting that public awareness becomes little more than political opportunism. Nothing ever gets done because no good crisis ever goes to waste within the minds of activists. Solutions may bring results, but results bring an end to political necessity. And political leaders prefer to keep his or her job and, therefore, problems *always* seem just beyond the reach of effective legislation.

Regardless, for every problem there *is*, in fact, a solution. Usually, too, this solution is very prominent and quite simplistic. Consider an obese individual for instance. The solution for his or her weight problem remains *discipline* in both eating and exercise. Eat less and exercise more remains the *only* way to effectively reduce body weight. Yet, billions are spent on wonder pills and "lose weight while you sleep" pronouncements. Similarly, legislatures pass laws ordaining obesity to be a handicap at best or a crippling disease at worst. At a minimum, businesses are sued or fined for not hiring people that are blatantly overweight. The "weight challenged" quickly become wards of the state.

If society cannot handle obesity without making it a national crisis, how are we supposed to tackle the concept of, say, abject evil? Of what "wonder pill" can eliminate another Rwanda tragedy or, even, Russia's subversion of Ukraine? What method exists by which sleep can silence Chicago's murder rate or stop thousands of illegal immigrants from flowing across the southern U.S. border?

The point is, there exists *no special tactic* that can defeat violence or aggression. No magic formula to end man's enduring inhumanity towards others. That said, perhaps the most effective measure to stop one from suffering a black eye remains to deliver a preemptive black eye in response. Or, in truest Biblical tradition, render that eye for an eye in measured response for those situations in which turning the other cheek seems fully impractical.

In Eastern culture, such symbolic reactions rarely made the headlines so to speak for they offered the world both Assassins and ninjas, two groups reared upon secrecy and covertness. They effected revenge through the dagger and poison; plied their trade following years of intimacy or servitude. Knowledge of their existence came by way of reputation and professional suddenness; rarely by fortuitous discovery. Theirs was a way of life rather than a method of operation.

Despite cultural differences, however, the West did offer the world Machiavelli and a host of other individuals eager to sway global politics through the sword and gunpowder. Others, from Washington on through Napoleon, understood the extreme value of espionage and intelligence; one handsomely victorious and the other notoriously defeated. Regardless, both the dagger and the cloak became synonymous with politics and power. If one could not sway the opposition, he simply eliminated that adversary for effect.

As global leaders became more accountable to their constituencies, the cloak gained preeminence over the dagger and so a world of intrigue and outright criminality flowed into the heretofore elitist world of politics. Soon, especially within liberal democracies, the theatrics of clandestine influence emerged as a full-time sport for those whose brilliance often masked his or her own lack of common sense and into this environment the modern covert paramilitary operative was born.

That secretive, non-military armies had been around for millennia does not diminish their spectacularism for the present. On the contrary, the advent of new technologies ensures that individual groups remain more lethal, able to hide within any terrain, cover their tracks expeditiously, and even engage within a range of social cover and concealment. In true force multiplication, a small party today could unleash more destruction than an entire legion of old – and do so without *anyone* knowing who orchestrated the attack.

| **Advantages** | **Disadvantages** |
| --- | --- |
| Secrecy ensures that the leaders behind the covert paramilitary operation remain undiscovered. | The same technology that permits secrecy also provides others with an opportunity to discover leadership. |
| Paramilitary forces allow for martial activity when military forces may not be an option. | Conventional military or covert paramilitary, aggression is *still* aggression and secrecy may simply aggravate the crisis. |
| Covert forces are generally specialized and cost-effective. | Paramilitary forces forfeit an opportunity for cross-training or extended mobilization. |
| Paramilitary forces, especially covert ones, can be more lethal than conventional militaries. | Lethality sometimes borders upon criminality and care must be observed when employing paramilitary forces. |
| Covert forces need not be authorized by legislature. | Operating outside legislatures remains grounds for impeachment or coups. |
| Professional, selective training remains extremely effective. | Murphy's Law always rears its ugly head in conflicts. |

Table 2. Advantages and disadvantages of Covert Paramilitary Operations.

Table 2 provides a brief analysis of the merits and demerits of covert paramilitary operations for consideration. For our discussion, we shall continue addressing these operations from their most practical manifestations, leaving the reader to understand that *anything* can go inherently wrong or that simple "dumb luck" may snatch victory from the proverbial jaws of defeat.

To remain practical, covert paramilitary operations *must* focus upon both the legitimacy and the rationality of their use. In other words, simply employing these groups to enhance political agendas will not work anymore than using them to sway foreign leaders. Clausewitz may imply that warfare is but an extension of political whims, but covert paramilitary forces must be used as a martial device to cease and defend against aggression while allowing aggression as an offensive option.

From here, we can determine some level of mobility, innovation, decentralization, and observational appreciation into their mix of lethality and psychological dexterity. As virtual standalone units, they can enter into areas – e.g., the aforementioned ungoverned spaces and hostile urban enclaves – hardened against more conventional (and observable) forces. As primarily covert operations, they can withstand the assaults of litigation and oversight that hamper their more traditional brethren.

However they may be employed operationally, covert paramilitary forces ensure an opportunity to engage an adversary on fundamentally different terms. In the case, say, of targeting trafficking or terrorist organizations, this permits the group to counter that enemy's violence with an even greater level of violence. In other words, when striking a hardened, vicious enemy, the best option always remains to kill with the utmost efficiency.

Here is where we must reiterate that covert paramilitary operations should not be left to the exclusive domain of tyrannical death squads or terrorist organizations. They represent a fundamental tool within the progress of *all* humanity as most elements of society – police, fire departments, etc. – began as purely private affairs prior to legislation turning these duties over to the public sector.

**Figure 2. SWAT units are fundamentally paramilitary organizations.** Image: © Martin Spurny - Fotolia.com

In Figure 2, we observe a highly trained SWAT unit from Europe. This team illustrates the professionalism, training, and discipline required for effective paramilitary operations, for their duties exceed that of conventional police forces and, yet, encompass more critical responses than most military organizations. Contrast this image with that presented in Figure 3 where the subject matter turns towards a less structured – but no means less lethal – paramilitary force consisting of two-man teams.

In this second case, we can assume a greater increase in operational security, mobility, and covert presence as *private* groups can achieve all three through methods fully denied to public, taxpayer-funded (and legislatively reviewed) forces. This reality is widely exhibited through the notoriety of Mexican drug "cartels".

**Figure 3. Private paramilitary teams offer challenges for military and law enforcement.** Image: © hurricane - Fotolia.com

Secrecy for criminal organizations translates simply into torturing, maiming, killing, or otherwise threatening members to remain silent – a vicious, but effective means of keeping things close to the vest.

In most cases, however, paramilitary operations succeed because they consist of individuals whose devotion and dedication to the 'team' ensure secrecy. That is, they remain internally regulated with only minor investigation from leadership. The best options, of course, remain a cross between that exhibited in Figure 2 and Figure 3. Avoidance, of course, should be taken against "rogue" or fully *independent* paramilitary operatives (see Figure 4).

**Figure 4. Independent paramilitary soldier supporting conventional forces.** © Oleg_Zabielin - Fotolia.com

The introduction of such 'independent' soldiers offers the opportunity for dissent within the ranks and opportunism under the command of greed. In this regard, perhaps, paramilitary forces should shy away from pure mercenary behavior. They serve a distinct, operational function and must not be clouded by opportunism or politicization as no lethal force should ever be.

Unlike the padded punch of a professional boxer, paramilitary forces deliver the precise strike of a mixed martial arts fighter. More specifically, paramilitary forces *should* deliver a singular crippling blow that will cause the other "fighter" to think twice about responding. To achieve this response, however, requires those employing paramilitary forces to *focus* their strikes and *ensure* that sufficient thrust is delivered. Partial attention never validates any activity, let alone ones that may bring about a large and massive counterstrike from conventional armies.

To survive – both martially and administratively – the best paramilitary forces must draw upon the stealth of ninjas, the patience of the Assassins, the endurance of Roger's Rangers (of 18th century fame), the resourcefulness of World War II's Chindits, and apply all that to 21st century technology and socialization. Confronting these forces, however, represent adversaries as every bit as primitive as that which beset humanity since Creation began.

The crises of the 21st century will offer a sharp dividing line between "Western Christianity", say, and "Pre-Christian" realities. That is, the stabilization and equality that existed throughout the world for the past 2,000 years will dissipate as the planet reenters the era of industrialized evil – including a total disregard for human life (of any age), the tragic destruction of the nuclear family, litigation as an offensive weapon, and the indiscriminate silencing of opposition. That much of this has already taken place during the past fifty years or so does not imply that the worst has already occurred.

In this regard, the reader can expect the following to occur within the next decade:

✓ An atrocity-centric battle between Progressives and Faith-based groups.

✓ Immigration will continue to soar from methodical, legal avenues towards massive "caravan type" invasions of other sovereignties as anarchists attempt to reengineer the political order.

✓ Human smuggling and drug trafficking (and local narcotics production) will take over smaller communities whose indigenous police forces will be unable to deal with the insurrection.

✓ The decimation of human integrity will permit larger governments to redefine concepts (e.g., gender identity, religious faith, education, etc.) that had heretofore withstood the tests of time.

✓ Social media and data communications will continue influencing youth faster than these individuals' minds will be able to challenge the data.

✓ Career politicians will continue to advocate majority vote to diminish representative legislatures permitting those who hold the purse strings of government to purchase votes over the needs of his or her constituencies.

✓ Public debts will continue to soar past sustainable levels ensuring that a fundamental battle will exist between the state and those who do not wish to become wards of the state.

- ✓ Feudalism and serfdom will begin to replace legitimate public authority as cronyism bears both the both and the funding to entice citizens.

- ✓ Major retailers such as Walmart and Amazon will break down as the public matures from addictive consumerism to entitled servitude leaving a strong void between those who *expect* to maintain comfortable lifestyles with little or no cost to themselves.

These "predictions" bear several factors in common.

First, as populations increase dramatically, public services will never be able to provide for the expectations of that convenience-driven society. Second, as people strive to consider "other" sources of pleasure and happiness, traffickers will flood in to fill their needs through drugs, sex, and a chance for a better life *somewhere*. Third, through online ordering and in-store personal shoppers, individuals will simply acquiesce to *others'* efforts and labors. Finally, politicians and other activists will take advantage of the situation to promote alternatives to the "failures" of what they proclaim as archaic, traditional systems of belief.

Tradition and experimentation remain on a collision course with no chance for an effective spur to sideline one or the other until reasonable debate can succeed. Politically, those who wish to retain honored traditions and those who seek to profit from the introduction of socialist programs, will never abdicate from his or her position. Historically, this suggests that only war – or open hostilities – will settle the outcome.

Into this mix of politics and privatization, trafficking

and socializing, profit and entitlement, rests the prospects for covert paramilitary forces operating within both legitimate and illicit capacity. These groups will carry the banner of "ghost wars" well into the century, perhaps even redefining the nature of humanity itself. Certainly, reexamining humanity's preferences in waging that conflict.

For the past 25,000+ years of organized "civilization", the only perennial loser has been governance itself, a victim of its own device. As people congregated into mutually agreeable patterns, they decided that the relative few could provide for the obvious many. In this regard, they first chose – then recruited – individuals that could serve as policemen, firefighters, judges, jailors, educators, and, of course, leaders. These became occupations, as much as had hunters, fishermen, and farmers, so that everyone could benefit from otherwise disagreeable industries. Yet people are not necessarily sociable.

There is an analogy to this within western Iowa, for instance. Corn subsidies and wind turbine energy have turned generational farmers into some of the wealthiest individuals around. This, in turn, drove up the price of housing as new construction rested with those whose ownership of the land dictated the existence of one's neighbors. As the farmers grew wealthier with less effort, the rest of citizenry had to accept menial labor within the area's few retailers. The dividing line between the 'haves' and the 'have nots' led many of the latter into despair, addiction, and poverty.

With no "middle class" to speak of, this area of the United States remains representative of many places around the world where the ladders of success disappear for all but those whose livelihood is largely bequeathed. The underlying similarities rests with very few law enforcement officials and empowering criminal elements. That the former is restricted through legislated doctrine and the latter unleashed through competitive adaptation (and mutual brainstorming) underscore the need for covert response.

Where communities remain far less democratic in nature they offer more militant clashes between the state and local governments and the violent criminal elements threatening those communities. Here is where covert paramilitary operations manifest themselves in a role where they are most ideally suited: clandestine termination of threats through the effective use of extreme violence.

More diverse than mere "hunter-killer" teams and less extrajudicial than "death squads", paramilitary forces govern that territory eluding both law enforcement and military units. From the more civilized perspective, they can provide security for a given region (though done more overtly), allowing medical supplies and food to reach threatened areas. From the more militant vantage, they can judiciously eliminate those individuals whose incarceration or subjugation remains nearly impossible.

Whatever their role, *effective* paramilitary operatives possess the initiative, discipline, training, and self-reliance that conventional military personnel lack. When used within a covert capacity, they provide the success and force multiplication that national (and some business) leaders only dream about. Again, their success rests upon *unrestrained asymmetrical warfare* in all its manifestations.

Psychologically, there is nothing more intimidating than a group that can strike anywhere it wants without fear of detection (e.g., the ninjas) or whose mere reputation sends adversaries catatonic with fright (e.g., the Assassins). That these individuals may not frequent the Internet or manipulate social media merely intensifies the notoriety of the ages.

Well-disciplined, "ghost soldiers" are literally – and,

perhaps, rightfully – glorified within Hollywood action films.

**Figure 5. The professional paramilitary is a force to reckon with.** © 1000words - Fotolia.com

They turn martial excellence into an art form, taking military science and practical necessity into levels unheard of within bureaucratic conventional forces. Their job is to influence through intimidation, tactics, and precision firepower when necessary (see Figure 5). That they can do all this with little or no exposure merely intensifies their mystique.

To avail oneself to all these merits requires a massive contribution for appreciation – as should be the case for *all* professional military personnel. As with a fine jeweler's tool, covert paramilitary operatives can be damaged through inattention, misuse, or negligence. As all tools of any trade, they exist to accomplish one purpose with extreme prejudice – the working of another 'object' into submission or value. In this context, covert paramilitary forces remain priceless for the task of rendering adversaries "unable to inflict harm".

## Summary

Covert, "secret soldiers" remain any government's most effective and lethal tool to impart its influence upon others, whether large standing armies or regional criminal enterprises. Nevertheless, they are often misused as "personal armies" or not employed within the strictest covert capacity, diluting their ability to perform where their talents best suggest. As the world migrates away from its relative fascination with taxpayer-funded conveniences towards a more traditional approach to social justice, the political Left and Right will drift further apart, leaving mainstream populations caught within a battle of ideologies. These micro wars will test the ability of conventional police and military forces, offering a pretext for further paramilitary operations undertaken both by governments and private entities.

R.J. Godlewski (Pronounced *GOD LES KEY*) is a freelance threat resolution services consultant specializing in irregular warfare and corporate security operations and the architect of Fourth-Generation Corporate Security (4GCS) doctrine. He holds an M.A. in Military Studies/Asymmetrical Warfare and a B.A. in Intelligence Studies/Terrorism Studies both of which earned with honors from American Military University where he further earned graduate and undergraduate certificates in Security Management and Explosive Ordnance Disposal, respectively. Mr. Godlewski is a veteran of the U.S. Navy and U.S. Navy Reserve and devotes his time to defending innocent human life from conception on through natural death. Whatever it takes...

## MORE BY R.J. GODLEWSKI...

*Supplemental Skills of the Assassin: Devil's Advocacy*

*Effective Hunter-Killer Operations*

*Independent Force Protection: Private Security for Preppers*

*Communities at War: Defending our schools, hospitals, and houses of worship in the 21st Century.*

*Practical Guerrilla Warfare*

*Explaining God: Ten Chapters to Introduce the Almighty to the Uninitiated*

*More Skills of the Assassin: Delving Deeper into Human Depravity*

*Mini-Manual of the Independent Counterterrorist, Third Edition*

*Fourth-Generation Corporate Security: Asymmetrical Warfare for Protective Services Professionals*

*Targeting Narco-Submarine Networks through Deep Penetration, Autonomous Maritime Irregular Warfare Units Operating within a Hunter-Killer Role*

*Of What Price, Heaven? Encountering God Within a Highly Secularized Society*

*Skills of the Assassin: Understanding the Tactics of the Professional Killer*

*Bogdan Back Flies and the Children of Desperation* (Fiction)

*Antevastatio Militis* (Fiction)

*The Gatestrian Knights* (Fiction)